SAVE YOUR *OWN* DAMN LIFE

A Do It Yourself Self Help Book

JESSICA JEBOULT

This book is dedicated to my family.
Thanks to this pack of stone cold weirdos for making me strong, independent and providing me with the best content ever!
I love you all!

Table of Contents

Introduction vii

Commitment No. 1
Body..2
Diet 15

Commitment No. 2
The Mind...29

Commitment No. 3
Connection 60
Connection to Yourself 63
Connection with Others 88
Connection to Something Bigger 100

Commitment No.4
Productivity 105

Resources 131

This Book Belongs to :

Introduction

Warning: This is not your typical self help book.

This is not a book with a picture of a lake and a dock in muted greens on the cover. This is not a book you use to commiserate and wallow in self pity with. This is a book of action. This is a book that is going to light a fire under your ass. This isn't a regular self help book, this is a cool self help book. It will educate, entertain and inspire you to save your own damn life, not just read about it.

This book will be your personal journey. I give you the framework and you apply the tools and strategies.

It works because you are filling in the blanks as you read along. This book is a partnership between me and you.

Now I know what you are probably thinking.

What in the heck is a "do it yourself, self help book?!" Well you are in for quite an adventure. Do you ever find yourself flipping through your regular self help books and thinking "Oh that's a good idea, I'm going to write that down." Only to never, ever write it down. Usually because there was no room or you completely forget. As a self help book junkie myself, I always did this. With every book I had these grand ideas of action and never pursued any of them and just kept on reading. This is where the do it yourself, self help book approach was born.

Gone are the days of wishing and hoping and praying. This is the only self help book you will ever need. I have been where you have been and it has taken me over ten years to break it all down. You don't have to wait ten years, you can figure it out today. I have the cheat codes to living a happy, healthy, productive life filled with love.

This isn't just theory, this book inspires change. I was always looking for outside sources to make me feel a certain way. I am here to tell you that you don't have to go to the deep forests of Peru to experience self development and connection. You don't have to have a shaman wave a feather over your head and drink some god awful tea to be considered healed.

Although those experiences sound lovely, they aren't necessary. Self help doesn't have to be so serious. It can be anything you allow and want it to be.

I am here to tell you that you can save your own damn life from the comfort of your own home. You can change your mindset, find a connection to yourself and live the life you have been dreaming about right where you are. You and only you are all you need to expand your personal development. You have everything you need buried inside of you and through this do it yourself, self help book I will help you uncover and tap into it.

Anxiety, Depression and Guilt.

I have been through it all. I have been where you are, I have felt and lived within these emotions. My addictions fueled these emotions to the point of debilitation.

Change is possible. I am living proof. I was living the fast life in the heart of Los Angeles, California. I was a full time traveling club Dj. I played all the big Hollywood parties in the hills and the hottest night clubs. I traveled to exotic places and partied with celebrities till the cows came home. On paper I had the perfect rockstar life. It was fun, until it wasn't. I found myself with no real relationships. No one I could really be real and honest with. I hated the hours. I was working while everyone was off having fun. I was shut off and shut down. I didn't want to be in clubs every night, having fake conversations with fake people. I was living this big life with nothing to show for it. It was all just stuff.

I was depressed because I wasn't fulfilled in my life, so I drank. I was anxious because I was depressed, so I drank. I felt guilty for not having motivation to change my life, so I drank.

I wanted to feel good. I was sick of feeling anxious, depressed and guilty. So I made a list of people, places, situations and things that made me feel good. I went through my life with a fine tooth comb and eliminated all the bullshit my ego was doing to be cool and traded it for things that made my soul sing. Just as you have to plan for success. You also have to plan for happiness. So stop doing shit that doesn't make you happy and feel good!

In this book you will learn the four commitments in order to Save Your Own Damn Life: Body, Mind, Connection and Productivity.

These four commitments are the source and foundation of everything. Every single day, every action and every experience we have, falls into one of the four commitments. Every goal, or dream we have fits within one of these four commitments. These are tools that you integrate into your life, they aren't steps.

Soon enough you won't even have to think about them because you will naturally adopt them into your daily routine. They are simple, effective and do not require anything fancy.

Just like a chair has four legs your framework for building out your best life has four commitments. When one of the legs on the chair is wobbly and isn't living up to its potential, things start to get shaky. You can track by the day, hour or minute what needs to be tightened up. What commitment needs some love to maintain a solid foundation.

I am not an educated doctor or a fancy scientist. I did not grow up with a silver spoon in my mouth, I'm not even a writer or author.

I'm not smarter or wiser than you are. I personally needed something to help me track, help me pivot and get me the results I wanted. That is why I created these four commitments.

If you want to take control of your life like I did, let's get to work!

Jessica Jeboult

ANYTHING I CAN DO, YOU CAN DO TOO.

Jessica Jeboult

Commitment No. 1

Body

> "To keep the body in good health is a duty...
> otherwise we shall not be able to keep the mind
> strong and clear."
> – Buddha

Seeing is believing. Since this is a transformational book that means there are going to be a lot of changes around here. Some you can see and some you can't and to some that can be scary. I absolutely understand your hesitation or cynicism, trust me I was where you are. I didn't believe anything unless it is staring me straight in the face.

To prove there is a method to my madness, let's start off with the physical. It's hard to gauge if things are changing or working if you can't physically see anything. It's like wifi, you know it's working and it's out there, but you can't physically see it. You just have to trust it's out there, sending your emails and working its magic so you can stream cat videos all day, everyday.

The two main things that keep your body in working order are diet and exercise. They go hand in hand, like Mickey and Minnie or the sun and moon. Having a steady fitness routine and eating healthy is not a luxury. It is vital. Being in good physical health is essential to your wellbeing as heat and electricity are essential to your home. Your body runs it all. Your body is what makes the action happen. Your body is what drives you to work, it's what hugs your family tight, it's what makes love to your partner all night long, or for a good, solid six and a half minutes. Your body is what gets you through each and every day.

This is a chance to commit to yourself and to your body. To get rid of the excuses. I know, I know everyone is busy and everyone works. Everyone has commitments to uphold. I get it, it's 2019 and if you're not busy you're considered dead or even worst, obsolete. But seriously, how busy are you going to be when you are laid up on bed rest from a heart attack because of your shitty diet and lack of exercise?

A healthy person has many wishes, but a sick person has only one.

How do you want to live your life? Do you want one wish or do you want endless possibilities? I can guarantee you that there are people that are busier than you and they fit in time to work out and take care of their body every single day. They do it because they are committed and you know what, commitment is sexy! You will either find a way or you will find an excuse. You choose.

I respect people who are committed to their body and their physique. Being physically fit is so much more than just looks. A well kept body is the ultimate status symbol. It is way hotter than a convertible Mercedes or big diamond earrings. Having a healthy body reflects a lot of hard work. Money can't buy it, you can't inherit it, you can't steal it, and you certainly can't borrow it. Trust me, I tried! The only way you can hold on to it is by maintaining it with constant, consistent work. A well kept body shows dedication, discipline, self respect, dignity, work ethic and passion for yourself. Being fit is far more than just looks, it shows your character without you saying a word or making a move.

When I see people at the gym at 5:30 am I think damn, now that's someone who honors and is dedicated to their health. To show that much commitment and putting in the hard work and doing whatever it takes, that is a turn on. It doesn't matter how you do it, just get it done. Go to the local park and do a circuit on the playground or sign up for a fancy high end gym. Like Nike said, Just do it.

If you are trying to find the motivation to go to the gym, I can assure you that you will be waiting for the rest of your life. I don't think anyone actually enjoys the reality of what it takes to engage in physical activity. I'm talking about the hard work, getting hot and sweaty or waking up early or even the drive to the gym. You are not alone. However, what everyone does enjoy is the aftermath. That rush of adrenaline mixed with a healthy dose of serotonin coursing through your body, knowing that you showed up with your A game and gave it your all. The chance to get into the zone, turn off your minds inner chatter, escape your screaming children and run your ass off to Madonna on the treadmill. That's the good stuff.

One side effect I noticed from working out was the more I did it, the better I felt about myself. The better I felt about myself the better I ate. The better I ate, the clearer and more present I became. One good decision becomes a good habit and that good habit developed into a good routine that in turn sparked even better decisions. All that goodness started to compound.

Do you see where I'm going here?

Don't Let the Sweat Pants Fool You

Whenever I feel unattractive or don't want to put in the mental bandwidth to getting dressed, I wear sweatpants. I choose them not only out of comfort but out of pure laziness. I work from home and for myself. It's hard to get motivated and really show up and show off when I am the only person there. I would lounge around in my sweat pants all day and found that I was less motivated and less focused. That in turn made me less productive.

I let my work out schedule and diet slide because I was in sweats all day and convinced myself I didn't have time to work out. I didn't realize how forgiving and accommodating sweatpants were to a few extra pounds. I have made it a hard rule that I must show up to my desk dressed as if I was going into the office. Think casual Friday, bra and underwear are a must.

EAT LIKE YOU
LOVE YOURSELF.

MOVE LIKE YOU
LOVE YOURSELF.

SPEAK LIKE YOU
LIKE YOURSELF.

ACT LIKE YOU
LIKE YOURSELF.

LOVE YOURSELF.

-UNKNOWN

One seemingly innocent wardrobe choice let me get away with packing on a few extra pounds. Not going to lie because of that stretchy waist band, I was also more prone to snacking. It was a bit of a free for all.

Want accountability? Jeans, trousers or any pant with some sort of structure are quick to keep you in check. Any pant with a buttoned waist band is there to keep you in line and lookin' fine.

Are you single? Want a better sex life? Work out. Take care of your body. When you look good you feel good. When you look good, you want to show off what you got and rightfully so! Get it girl!

Work out and eat like you love your body. Treat your body like it was a special lover you haven't seen in a long time and your goal is to whisk them off their feet. Chances are you would feed them the freshest, most delicious, healthy meal that would nourish their body. You would wrap them up in your arms and caress their body with love and respect. Treat your body like you treat your long lost lover. The best part is, they aren't lost! You are your own special lover, so let's get to woo'ing!

Let Me Hear Your Body Talk

Let's talk about how we carry our beloved body. How we move through this world, and what our body language communicating to those around us. Body language is the unspoken element of communication. We use gestures, facial expressions and especially posture, to reveal our true feelings and emotions

My dog Ross is a constant reminder of how effective and impactful body language is. Because he can't speak english, just yet, we are working on it, his mannerisms and body language is how he communicates.

Most of the time he has his head down sniffing for treats or anything somewhat edible on the ground. He will eat anything and everything that isn't nailed down. With his head fixated on the ground, his tail at half mast, he does not want to be bothered, he's in his zone. His body language and posture changes instantly when he sees something he wants or is curious about.

For instance the neighborhood squirrel that lives in the tree in our front yard, he wants to get him, probably not to kill him but he definitely wants to smell him and see what his deal is. When a lady with a high pitched voice starts squealing at the sight of him, Ross saunters over to get loved on. Whenever Ross wants something his head is up, his ears are perked and his chest is puffed out and standing at attention. He transforms from homeless garbage dog to runway model chic in half a second.

When we are able to "read" these signs, we can use them to our advantage. Much like Ross, it can help us to understand the complete message of what someone is trying to say to us, and to enhance our awareness of people's reactions to what we say and do. We can use it to adjust our own body language so we appear more positive, engaging and approachable.

What does your body language say about you?

How do you communicate with your body? Are you a hand talker or a finger pointer? Do you stand up straight or like to slouch with your tail between your legs?

Where do you look when you speak to people, up down, all around?

One thing, amongst many, I learned from those handy dandy psychology courses, is that where you look when you are speaking to someone says a lot about you and your mental state. Where your eyes land is a major non verbal cue. It is like a cursor on a computer, it indicates what part of your brain you are using.

If you direct your gaze upwards, towards the ceiling or sky you are trying to visualize. If you are trying to think back to a memory or picture a storefront or intersection, taking your gaze upwards will help you tap you into visualizing mode. Your eyes are up and away and not able to maintain eye contact or it is somewhat strained when you are speaking to others.

By looking downwards toward the floor or below waist height, you are processing in your emotions, feelings and internal conversations. This is not the ideal place to be operating from. Most of the time when your eyes are down so is your head, both physically and mentally. Your chin is down, you are not able to make eye contact, and the body language you are giving off is saying closed, come back never.

Side note: Generally speaking this is how most people move through their day. This is the common stance for someone looking at there phone, constructing text messages, watching cat videos and scrolling through Instagram. Eyes down, head down. I wonder if this is why we take social media personally when our brains are operating in the emotional state.

Starring straight ahead and the eyes are moving side to side at ear level, is when you are thinking in words, sounds or music. You are pulling from your auditory senses and auditory memories. This is the ideal place to be looking. By "keeping your chin up," you are tapping into both the logical and emotional side of your brain and increase the ability to be present. Your body language is saying I am open for business, please come in.

Standing up straight, head up, eyes forward and making eye contact, is a very vulnerable position. Think back to a time when you were upset and had to have a conversation and communicate with someone. What was your body language like? Chances are when there were hard parts of the conversation you looked away and even looked down. This is a knee jerk reaction from our body to protect us. Our body wants to protect us from the reaction and help us find comfort in these uncomfortable, highly emotionally charged situations.

Take public speaking or making a presentation for instance. Being on a stage with lights, cameras and hundreds, maybe even thousands of people in the audience with all eyes on the presenter. That is very vulnerable position to be in. Have you ever seen someone delivering their speech with their head and eyes looking down to the ground? No way!

Their body language would instantly drive a wedge between them and the audience. There would be a huge disconnect because of the speakers body language. The same goes for you and how you move through the world and how you interact with others using your body. You don't need to be on a stage or have thousands of eyes on you to feel the same rush of emotions.

However, you do have to be mindful of the body language you are displaying. It is hard to be vulnerable but making tweaks to how you physically interact with others can make or break your connections and relationships.

I always had trouble looking people in the eyes. I felt if we made eye contact long enough they would be able to see into my soul. If we locked eyes for more than a minute this person was going to see the chaotic tornado that was swirling around in my brain, sucking up everything in its path and spitting it out on the other side. This was terrifying. When your soul is in a state of absolute crap, you don't want anyone looking at it!

Being physically open and vulnerable allowed me to become emotionally vulnerable. If you are a tough nut to crack, like myself, this is a great way to dip your toe in the vulnerability pool. Follow this check list to become more physically vulnerable in your day to day life.

1. Eye check:

Where are you looking? Eyes up, chin up. Do this even when you don't want to. Raising your gaze up even a few inches can raise your mood.

2. Posture check:

Roll your shoulders back, down and away from your ears. Stand up straight and present your beautiful body to the world.

3. Mind your limbs:

Are your arms and legs crossed like a human pretzel? Open them up. Unravel your limbs. You can't run and jump into a loving embrace with your legs tangled up with each other.

Fashion, Fashion, Fashion!

What we wear and how we choose to express ourselves through our clothing is another form of body language. What you wear and how you wear it says a lot about how you view yourself. The garments you wrap around your body have said a thousand words before you have had a chance to say one. From sweat pants to a couture gown, every piece of clothing is an expression of a piece of you.

I was the princess of darkness. I would smother myself in black. I was constantly on the hunt for a color darker than black. It was my uniform. It was easy, edgy and described exactly how I was feeling inside. All in all I was dark. I felt dark and cold on the inside and I wore it on the outside. From the looks of it, you would have thought I was some gothic, punk rock kid. Close, I was just an emotionally unstable, drowning in my own sorrows, going through an identity crisis girl in my mid twenties. No biggie.

I liked black so much, I went as far as to color my hair dark, dark, almost black, chestnut brown. I am a natural blonde and for 12 years I insisted on staining my beautiful, bright, golden locks a dark deep, moody brown. I was covering up my natural glow. I looked like a completely different person. I looked hard and cold and very uninviting. I didn't want to open myself up or let anyone in and my "look" made sure of that.

It wasn't until I began to save my own damn life that everything changed. I lightened my hair and went back to my natural blonde. I felt like a weight had been lifted. I was no longer this sharp, dark crow. I had transformed into a bright colorful butterfly. I also added colored pieces into my wardrobe and haven't been able to stop. The joy and excitement I get from wearing a bright t-shirt or colored pants, is positively shocking.

I am not the only one. I met a man who wore nothing but white. We met when I was volunteering at a farm in Malibu. When I asked him why he wore all white he explained that he was in the dark for so long. He was a recovering addict who had been in a motorcycle gang and jail most of his life. He would wear all black, all the time. Black leather jackets and vests that weighed on his body, with black pants and black shit kickin' boots. Black on black was a way of life. "I was in a very dark place for most of my life, everything I did I wanted to cover up and black it out."

Today I wear white for freedom. I am free both literally and figuratively. "I don't fear the impending doom of my actions and wearing all white symbolizes how light I feel knowing that."

Shedding that deep, dark weight of clothing and hair color was a transformation in itself. How we present ourselves on the outside can change and reflect how we feel on the inside. Try lightening up your wardrobe, literally. Wear lighter, brighter colors and see how that effects your mood.

Raising yourself up and choosing to treat your body like the temple that it is will start to trickle down to other parts and situations in your life. Before you know it you start having better days, that compound into better weeks, that builds out into better months and so on. By taking care of your body it will help prime you to make good choices for yourself, and that is what this sweet thang called life is all about, choices.

"TAKE CARE OF YOUR BODY. IT'S THE ONLY PLACE YOU HAVE TO LIVE."

JIM ROHN

Diet

Choosing to take care of your body through diet and exercise is directly connected to saving your own damn life. If you want a better life, get in better shape. It doesn't matter where you are at in your life, not taking care of your body and eating poorly is just inexcusable.

We have the luxury to choose whatever we want to eat. Think about that. At this very second you have the option to either go to the grocery store, order something from an app on your phone or go to a restaurant and get whatever the hell you want.

We no longer have to go out and hunt and gather our food. We aren't foraging for our meals, heck we are barely cooking our own these days. We are in a position to feed ourselves how we want, when we want and what we want.

If we are no longer in a state of survival why do you we choose to eat crap. Put it this way you wouldn't put regular gas in a Lamborghini. A Lambo needs the highest grade fuel out there and so do you. Stop treating your body like a 1995 Ford Fiesta. You are a high end luxury vehicle and you need to start treating and loving yourself that way. You put good in, you get good out.

Every time I put crap into my body I feel like I am dulling myself down. If my physical body is a sword, I strengthen and sharpen my sword every time I work out and eat healthy. With every yoga class or homemade salad I put into my body I run my sword along a sharping stone, making me sharper and able to cut through life with ease.

Eating crappy food is like cutting through life as a butter knife. All you can do is spread shit around. And don't even think of cutting things with it. You are round and dull. Nothing sharp about you. Have you ever tried to cut a tomato with a butter knife? It is not pretty! You end up with shards of half cut, mushed and mutilated tomato. That is exactly how your body becomes when you pump it full of unhealthy foods and try to demand something it isn't physically capable of.

The food you ingest affects you both physically and mentally. If you think that processed, fatty foods full of unpronounceable words don't affect your body and state of mind you have another thing coming, sister. Food is used to nourish your body. You put your body through so much mentally and physically, your diet should be there to replenish and empower your body, not make it work harder to digest ungodly, unnatural chemicals. Eating healthy and being mindful of what you put in your body is showing your body love and compassion. It is the highest form of self care and self respect.

Brace yourself I'm going to get all scientific on you.

It is said by doctors and other smart people in white coats, that the gut is your second brain. It holds all your emotions and feelings. Like the saying goes, "Trust your gut," or "I have knots or a pit in my stomach." Those feelings are all related to your emotions. Your brain may be warning and telling you something, but your gut is feeling and cultivating those emotions. That being said you can literally change your mood by what you ingest. You are what you eat is very literal.

The enteric nervous system is a mesh-like network of neurons that lines the entire digestive tract. It causes the sensation of nervous butterflies or a pit in your stomach that are innate parts of our psychological stress responses. Up to 90 percent of the cells involved in these responses carry information to the brain rather than receiving messages from it, making your gut as influential to your mood as your head is. Maybe even more.

Did you know that 95% of your bodies serotonin is found in your bowels? Doctors are finding the need to expand to treat the second brain in addition to the one on top of your shoulders. By practicing healthy eating habits this allows you to be in the driver seat to your emotional well being. Not only is diet and exercise relative to your appearance it's a key player in your mental health.

Again, with all these facts and knowledge, why do we keep eating and drinking things we know are bad for us? Some foods have stronger bonds to us than we even realize. The term comfort food is alive and well. You know those certain meals that with one whiff you are transported back in time. My catalogue of comfort food is vast and deep. Food is so much more than what I am eating, it is an experience chalk full of feelings and emotions that can be both positive and negative.

Our emotional connection to what we eat and drink is so strong all the logic in the world can't define it, because it's not logical at all, it's emotional. One particular meal that comes to mind is "Danny's Chicken." My mom makes it and it is one dish that every single person in my family absolutely loves. Everyone is instantly in a great mood, regardless of what happened in their day. When they hear or smell that "Danny's Chicken" is on the menu it lifts everyone's spirits.

Right off the bat that's a pretty strong emotional connection. One single dish that has the power to bring my whole family together and in a positive way? That must be a friggin' miracle. Danny's Chicken is not your typical meat and potato meal. This is a curry based dish, which for my family is a stretch for their palates. That is what makes this whole experience even more unique. When I think about Danny's chicken I instantly get a smile on my face and my mouth starts to water. I can taste the curry and the broccoli in the creamy sauce and I am instantly transported to my family dinner table.

I have tried to replicate this meal hundreds of times. I have used the same recipe, same ingredients and it just doesn't feel the same. I am never satisfied and left with an aching emptiness that's still there even after I have finished the whole pan! So what's missing? Because this meal has such a strong emotional connection ingrained in me, no matter how I prepare it, how much I eat, I will never be satisfied because I am missing the most important ingredient. The one not on the recipe list and certainly not available at any store, the love of my family and the emotions I have wrapped up in Danny's Chicken.

This is true for so many of the foods and drinks we eat. This can be positive or negative. Remember that time you got sick and threw up ramen noodles and vowed to never eat ramen again because of that experience and emotional connection? Same thing. So how do we break or harness these emotional connections?

First things first, you need to recognize them. Once you realize "Oh I am drinking or eating this because it makes me feel this." That is when you can begin to separate and distinguish the emotional aspect of the food you are eating and the drinks you are drinking.

Most peoples vices are comfort foods. Mac and Cheese, your mom's lasagna, pizza, you get the idea. No ones initial reaction when you say comfort food is a salad. That is because these fatty comfort foods have imprinted positive emotions on our minds and we think that if we ingest them we will feel better and everything will be ok. We long for those warm fuzzy feelings by stuffing our faces with what is familiar and comfortable.

Danny's Chicken

This is really easy and your family and loved ones will love it!

3 Boneless chicken breasts

1/4 tsp Pepper

3 Tbsp Oil

2 Heads of Broccoli

1 10oz can of Cream of Chicken Soup

1/2 cup Mayonaise

1 tsp Curry powder

1 tsp Lemon juice

1 Cup Grated cheddar cheese

Cut chicken into bit sized cubes and sprinkle with pepper. Sauté slowly in oil over medium heat until white (about 6 minutes). Cook broccoli until tender. I put it in a microwave safe bowl with water and put it in the microwave for about 5 minutes. Drain water and arrange broccoli at the bottom of a casserole pan. Place chicken on top of the broccoli. Mix soup, mayonnaise, curry and lemon juice together. Pour mixture over the broccoli and chicken and top with shredded cheddar cheese.

Bake uncovered at 375 F for 30-35 minutes. Serves 4-6 . Spread it on top of rice or quinoa.

The most dangerous comfort food I craved was alcohol. My deep seeded connection was so strong it became a need. Alcohol and I were so wrapped up in our emotional relationship we became very codependent. I was convinced I needed alcohol and drugs to be the person I wanted to be. That my ideal self only came out when I was drinking. Now that's a pretty scary place to be. I wasn't fun, cool, outgoing or pretty enough. I wasn't the life of the party or star of the show without my partner in crime.

I didn't see the point. I didn't see any reason for someone to want to be around me or get to know me if I wasn't drunk or if I didn't have booze or drugs to share. I was never good enough on my own. My emotional connection with alcohol and drugs was so powerful I never and could never imagine my life without it. There was no possible way I could *not* drink. The very thought of having a conversation with someone without a drink in hand was not an option.

I found comfort in this person I had become. It was familiar and predictable. I knew how I would feel and who I would become once I got that buzz I longed for. That warm fuzzy feeling that I thought made me whole. Essentially I was chasing that same feeling of Danny's Chicken. Instead of trying to find it in a curry chicken dish, I was trying to find it in the bottom of a champagne bottle, or four.

I didn't realize that this emotional connection and co dependency with alcohol and then drugs was ruining my life. When alcohol wasn't fulfilling my needs we added a third to our relationship to spice things up, cocaine. My body was breaking down physically. I was always sick. Every single time I went home for the holidays I would never make it to family activities and became known as a flake. My body was so run down and exhausted from the bender I just went on the night before with old high school friends, I could barely muster up the energy to change the channel on the TV. I had traveled all the way home to spend time with my family for the holidays but because of what I chose to put into my body, I made it physically impossible to show up.

I chose to drink like a fish. I chose to snort lines till 8 am. I did this all because this is how I related to others and most of all to myself. I thought this was the only possible way to show up and live out who I always wanted to be or thought I could be. In fact I was doing the complete opposite of my so called life goals. I had this emotional connection and thought I needed drugs and alcohol to be the fun, bubbly person I always aspired to be and it was sucking the life out of me.

I looked like death. Straight up looked like a member of the Cullen's vampire family from the Twilight movies. I was so pale, I was practically transparent. Not only did I look sick, I was a sick person. I was poisoning my body and it showed. I looked 10 years older than I was because the alcohol and drugs were sucking every ounce of moisture from my body. My skin was crusty and dehydrated. No amount of night cream, face masks or botox can revive skin that looks and has the texture of turkey jerky.

That type of hydration is only fixable from the inside. My body was beyond dehydrated. My nose and entire nasal cavity was dryer than the Sahara desert. I would get nose bleeds that would last for up to an hour. Another super cute side effect to cocaine was that my septum became extremely deviated. Other wise known as "coke nose." That is a medical term by the way. So if the nosebleeds weren't cute enough add on a face that looks like Picasso painted it with a half collapsed nose.

Whoever says drugs and alcohol don't affect your body, is a liar liar pants on fire. After being physically sick for many years I started to see my connection to alcohol and drugs in a new way. My emotional connection was beginning to see the light of day and I realized I had to dump and sever this relationship asap. I always looked to alcohol to gain something from it. Whether it was more energy, to be more outgoing, to have more fun, more of this or more of that. What I didn't realize was it was taking way more than it was giving.

At the end of the day I was sick and tired, grumpy and depressed. I was exactly the opposite of all the qualities I had wrapped up and connected to alcohol and drugs. Turns out alcohol and drugs are liars and they didn't have a leg to stand on when I confronted them. Everything I ever wanted was already inside me. And guess what, once I stopped drinking I was pretty enough, smart enough and fun enough all on my own.

The trick to releasing foods or anything we don't want is to replace it with something we do want. My goal was to be a happy, loving, bubbly, light person. So how could I achieve that when I am hanging out in dark bars, blacking out and getting verbal and physically abusive with people I loved? We need to replace these connections with healthier options. Quitting without a viable substitute or alternate options, is leaving a lot of room for error.

It is like getting into a cab and the driver asks where you want to go and you say, "Well I don't want to go to the park." Focus on what you want. What do you want your life to look like? How do you want to feel? Those are two very powerful questions that can be applied to any subject in your life. If what you are putting into and what you are doing with your body doesn't make you feel good, its time to change that.

What in your life can you replace with a healthier option?

How can you make your favorite comfort food dishes with healthier ingredients. Can you replace your moms spaghetti with spaghetti squash or zucchini noodles as pasta? What about the sugar department. Do you consume sugar like an elf from the north pole? What are healthier options you can implement into your diet?

Use the chart to make a list of foods you want to swap out and replace with healthier options. By making these little changes, you will reap big rewards. Remember you have the power to choose what you put into your body, so make sure its good stuff!

Replace this:
Soda

With that:
Sparkling water

Self discipline and commitment will set aside the people who get shit done and those who just talk about getting shit done. Change is relatively easy, it's commitment that demands work. You need to do this for you and you alone. I can't think of one positive outcome that has come from being unhealthy. Not one. Treat your body with respect and honor it like the temple it is. Make a commitment to loving your body inside and out with a solid fitness and diet plan.

Follow these steps to complete the first commitment to saving your own damn life:

1. Hire a trainer/find a work out partner:

Immediately.

Not tomorrow or when you have more time or money. Make time. If you don't have the funds available right now look for less expensive options. There are community centers and inexpensive work out facilities. You can find trainers anywhere. Everyone has a friend, or a friend of a friend who's a trainer. Your local gym can recommend someone to you as well.

Having a trainer or a work out partner keeps you accountable. Trainers are there to make your fitness and diet goals easier. They are trained and educated, so let them tell you what to do. A work out partner is another option if a trainer isn't in the cards.

Pick a work out partner carefully. Go with someone who is already fit and eats well. Watch and study what they do and make adjustments to create your own plan. Emulate someone that has something you want. This will push you. If you go with a friend that's lazy, guess what you will be lazy. I used to go to the gym with a friend that considered briskly walking on the tread-mill for 20 minutes while talking, texting and taking selfies on her phone a "killer workout." Crazy co-ordination skills, yes, a killer workout, absolutely not!

2. Diet

Get rid of all your shitty food.

Put this book down and clean out all the crap food you have in your cupboards. I'm talking about the candy, chips, and all that processed junk. All of it must go now. If you're going to make some real changes, start now.

Eating healthy isn't expensive, but being overweight and sick is. Hire a nutritionist or ask your trainer for meal plans. Eating healthy is not a diet or a fad, it is a way of life. There are count-less resources to find guidelines for healthy eating. There are apps on your phone and meal delivery services with specific eating plans. You must be committed to this every single day. There is no excuse for not working out and eating healthy and having a body that can do whatever you tell it to do.

3. Commit

Make a commitment right now to having a plan for tomorrow. Write down exactly when, (morning, afternoon, after work) and where you will work out tomorrow.

What exercises you will do and your plan going forward. Are you going to hire a trainer or find a work out partner? Where are you going to shop for your groceries? What healthy meals can you prepare for yourself ?

Be specific about what changes and commitments you will make to take care of your body. Nothing bad can come from exercise and eating healthy.

Make the commitment, you're worth it.

If you fail to plan, you plan to fail. Write out your plan of action for your diet and exercise goals.

_____

_____

_____

_____

_____

_____

_____

_____

_____

_____

_____

Doctors won't make you healthy.

Nutritionists won't make you slim.

Teachers won't make you smart.

Gurus won't make you calm.

Mentors won't make you rich.

Trainers won't make you fit.

Ultimately, you have to take responsibility.

Save yourself.

Commitment No. 2

The Mind

"The mind is not a vessel to be filled but a fire to be kindled" -Plutarch

Every single action and emotion starts in the mind.

Love

Attraction

Sex

Fear

Doubt

Anxiety

From the choices we make to the emotions we feel. Your mind is a garden and your thoughts are the seeds you plant. What it grows is 100% up to you. You are responsible for your thoughts. If you do nothing with your mind, never study, never learn and never expand or increase your skill set, it will bring forth weeds. If you fail to manage the garden, the weeds will take over and undesirable things will grow.

Drama, fear, doubt, hesitation, resentment, lies, negativity. Are all like an annoying mosquito that just insists on buzzing away right by your ear at 2:30 am while you are trying to sleep. If you cannot control and discipline your mind, your anger and fear will show up every time and won't stop buzzing.

If you cannot control and discipline your mind, you will never create a consistent, effective workout routine. If you cannot control and discipline your mind, your business will never be consistent and your income will be impacted. If you cannot control your mind your emotions will be hijacked by anyone and anything you come in contact with. If you plant good seeds, manage the weeds, and harvest good crops by watering, nourishing and pruning the garden of your mind, you can inject positivity. You can instill knowledge, and tools that allow you to create a garden that will flourish and bloom.

The mind is a glorious creature. It has ways of lifting us up and dropping us flat on our asses. Our thoughts are not reality. Inside our head, between our ears is an internal voice that is constantly spewing information, sometimes facts, sometimes fiction. That is where the tricky part comes in. It's up to us to decipher which thoughts are which. How do you determine if a plant is a flower or a weed?

Growing up my inner voice was so controlling and over bearing in my day to day life, I gave up. From a very young age I let myself be bullied by my inner saboteur. Her name is Debbie, Debbie Downer. Her voice was the one who enforced all the limitations. If there was joy to be had Debbie could smell it from a mile away. She would rev up the ol' guilt and self sabotage talk like she was about to drag race a 1970 Dodge Charger in The Fast and the Furious. Pressing her foot on the gas harder and harder, my inner voice grew louder and louder. Debbie's purr would turn to a loud roar in less than 60 seconds. That has to be some kind of record.

It became my form of communication, not just with myself but with the world around me.

Debbie's voice and influence became so loud the only way I knew how to cope with her was to drown her. I drowned her and the shame, anxiety and depression I was feeling with alcohol. The constant chatter of you aren't good enough, you aren't pretty enough, you aren't successful enough, aren't straight enough, you aren't gay enough, was too damn much.

I had let the real poison take over. Sure, to the naked eye alcohol and drugs were the obvious source of poison. But the real poison was my thoughts. I had no idea how to deal with Debbie and all these pent up emotions because I never learned how to control and harness my mind. Debbie won every damn time. I didn't stand a chance.

As a child I was too busy taking care of myself to explore my emotions and feelings and what to do with them. As the oldest of three children I assumed the role of the big sister and then some. My parent's had their hands full. As if parenting three kids wasn't hard enough, my youngest brother had a rare form of cancer in his eyes called retinoblastoma.

Between constant trips to Children's Hospital for tests and treatments and my parents marriage being on the rocks, there wasn't much room for anything else. My youngest brother was the main focus. You can't blame my parent's, they had a very sick kid on their hands. But what ended up happening was I never got the attention I needed as a child. I was too busy playing adult, independent Jessica and never got a chance to be a kid. I never had a chance to acknowledge or question my emotions because I never had a chance to explore or feel safe.

I did the worst thing you could do. I never talked. I never talked about Debbie, my thoughts or feelings, nothing. Didn't say a word. I thought this type of self talk was completely normal and that everyone mentally beat the living daylights out of themselves. No, just me? Cool.

No one talked about what was going on with my youngest brother and no one talked about my parent's divorce. Debbie and I were left alone to our own devices to fill in the blanks. No one talks about divorce. Like ever. Not when it was taboo and certainly not now because it's become so normal. It is expected that your parents will eventually get divorced and you are treated like some kind of unicorn when your parents are together. Either way, not talking is not good. By not talking and vocalizing my thoughts and feelings I just gave Debbie more fuel to continue on into my adult life.

I always came off angry. I was so serious and in my head trying to figure out what to do and what I have done wrong. I thought that in order to make something of myself or do something with my life I had to suffer. I had to work hard and don't even think about enjoying myself because successful people don't have fun. They are happy when they are successful but they certainly don't have fun when they are in the midst of becoming successful. I always had this idea that suffering meant I was working hard. If I was stressed and busy, I would by default be happy and successful, someday.

Momma >

Text Message
Today 3:07 PM

"I am lazy and have nothing to show for myself. It is really annoying, and I remember Dad doing this, I always try to find the easy way out. Sometimes I am so disappointed in myself. I remember when I was younger and Dad painted the upstairs bathroom. He couldn't be bothered to move things so he just painted around them. I feel like I have done this with my whole life."

So I did just that. I allowed Debbie to over ride and hijack my mind. My suffering would soon bring success, right? Once I had paid my dues and was stressed out to the max, worried and anxious about everything, that meant I cared or really wanted something.

Not too long ago I texted my mom, or should I say Debbie texted my mom. I had a stressful day to say the least and I let Debbie get the best of me. I was so low and heavy I could feel the weight in my fingertips as I texted her how I was feeling.

Since I was 12 years old my mom and I have always communicated through writing. We are both pretty emotionally charged people and nothing would be said or heard for that matter, if we didn't change our medium of communication. Keeping and passing along notes and sharing journals to write each other in is how we have communicated. This was my message to my mom. As you can see Debbie was 100 percent running the show. This message is Debbie in her finest form and is by far some of her best work. She has pulled in real life situations from the past, delicately woven them into the present situation and mixed in my current emotions making them feel like the truth. Your inner saboteur will stop at nothing to convince you of your failures and amplify those negative feelings, that's their job. No matter how strong, successful or accomplished you are, these thoughts exist in everyone's mind.

Just because they exist doesn't mean they are true. As you can see Debbie tried to pull one over on me. I am not lazy and I am definitely not a disappointment. My mom reminded me of all I have done in my life and continue to do on a daily, and hourly basis. I am anything but lazy. But in my moment of weakness that was my perspective and my truth.

I took Debbie's mind fuck challenge and raised her one. If Debbie thinks she can come at me full force, I will give it right back to her. For every time she said I was lazy, I countered her and challenged her. I wrote out what I had accomplished and how badass and grateful I am.

Before I knew it we were in a full on emotional negotiation. Spoiler alert, I have trained myself to win. Not soon after I plead my case, Debbie's voice became non existent. I couldn't hear her, not even a whisper of self doubt. Success! I have tamed the dragon once again. Put that in your pipe and smoke it, Debbie! All joking aside, I take this as a major win. Being at war with your own mind is a special kind of hell. In the past I would have suffered.

The child version of myself would have let Debbie wave her freak flag all over the place. Talking about her and acknowledging Debbie, takes her power away. She no longer has a warm, comfy place in my mind to set up shop. Vocalizing how I am feeling makes Debbie uncomfortable. The more uncomfortable she is the less likely she is going to stick around.

Name it to tame it

By recognizing when my inner critic is in the driver's seat and using a name for that piece of my mind, helps to process these feelings and emotions. It allows for disconnection from an emotionally convoluted state and allows some breathing room. Who is running your inner monologue? What would you name your inner saboteur?

Let's make it official! Fill out the name tag and call out your inner voices name.

Tell me more. Describe your inner voice. Write down every-thing about them. What they look like, how they dress. Their mannerisms, their attitude and phrases they say. Think of this as an online dating profile for your inner critic.

Building your emotional intelligence helps you to celebrate your highs and save those memories and content to your emotional spank bank. An emotional spank bank is when you can save those positive thoughts and feelings and go back and use them as a reference point and to help you inject an attitude of gratitude into your current emotional state. You can use these memories to get you off emotionally, it's like an elevated gratitude list. You not only have an emotional connection you also have a real life experience to reference.

Building this awareness to your emotions also helps you to process and constructively move through your emotional lows. Instead of having extreme peaks and valleys, you can maintain an ebb and flow to your emotions and in turn your reactions. By harnessing your mind you are cultivating and exercising healthy reactions.

You will be mentally prepared when you are running late to drop your kids off and someone cuts you off in traffic. Or when someone is on their phone and driving like a Hollywood jack ass. It won't grind your gears and have you flying off the handle in a fit of rage and you won't end up following them for the next ten blocks, just to pull up beside them to give them the much deserved middle finger. Ya those type of reactions.

First off, reacting like this is unproductive and a waste of your time. You are never going to resolve anything. Secondly, overreactions cause your adrenaline to raise and causes your body more stress and aggravation and that leads to more, you guessed it, stress and aggravation.

Thirdly, if you chose to over react, congratulations you are now way beyond late and you scared the shit out of your kids because you were driving way too fast and spilled their juice all over the back seat. I'm not one to dish out parenting advice but I think this is not the parent you should aspire to be.

Long story short, losing your shit gets you nowhere and actually further from where you want to be. So tell your inner voice, demon lady, sally sabotage, whatever you call her, to chill bra.

Speaking of chill, my Dad had absolutely no chill. None, zero, zip, nada. At any slight inconvenience my Dad would turn into Hulk Hogan, ripped shirt and all. For example, my little brother and I had just got out of my Dad's car and were about to cross the street when some dude in a pick up truck blew past us. Was he speeding yes, were we in a little bit of danger sure, was this a time to over react, absolutely not. My Dad started running after the guy in the pick up truck, yelling and screaming every curse word under the sun. When my Dad realized the truck was going too fast and he wasn't going to catch up to him to give him a piece of his mind, my Dad thought it was a great idea to throw his keys at the truck. Well, because it was a pickup truck with an open bed, you can only imagine where the keys landed. Yes, that's right, in the bed of the pick up truck. The driver sped on down the road with my Dads keys in the back.

Not only were we scared of being run over by a speeding driver, my brother and I were now subjected to our Dad with no chill, yelling and screaming like a lunatic. We learned new cuss words (which could be good or bad depending on how you look at it) and we were now locked out of the house because the keys, well as you know, were now in the back of some guys pickup truck.

"You have to train your mind to be stronger than your emotions or else you will lose yourself every time."

I have definitely always had what people would call "mood swings," because I am a girl and girls are emotional and dramatic. I hope you sense my sarcasm. I would always have extreme shifts in mood and the downward shift in particular was extremely taxing on me. It's like my mind hit the basement floor and found a trap door. I go low. I am speaking in present tense because I still have bouts of this feeling called depression. I don't believe it really goes away.

For years my depression ran wild and free. I had no clue or had any rhyme or reason to why or what was happening in my mind. I tried medication and that worked for a bit but eventually I had to up my dosage and it just felt wrong. All the medication did was make my mind fuzzy. It dulled not only my feeling of sadness and depression but all my feelings, even the good ones. It was like putting a filter over a bright shiny rainbow and making it muted, flat, and boring. It sucked.

I began to track my depression. I recorded when I felt the darkness rolling in and what was happening or not happening in my life. Any situations or altercations that came up I wrote them down. Depression is my inner voice on steroids. It's a nasty beast and has stronger powers than Debbie Downer. For me it is what happens when I don't curb Debbie and put her in her place when she starts talking shit. I have learned to recognize and manage what pushes me over the edge and when I just can't rein Debbie in.

A huge trigger for me is the feeling of being alone. The funny thing is this feeling can happen even if I am surrounded by people. It's a combination of connection and expectations I have wrapped around people and myself. That feeling of disappointment when those expectations aren't fulfilled within connections. It is an overwhelming sense of loss.

I never understood people who were so free flowing and easy going. You know the type of people who are so whimsical and say things like, " Ohh whatever happens is meant to happen, just let it be" type people. They fly by the seat of their pants. Ya that was not me at all. I was a control everything, everyone, every situation all the time. I work hard and think hard about everything and everyone until shit happens type person. I held every idea that floated into my mind with an iron fist. Some may call that perseverance, no it was actually bordering obsession.

I would get so down on myself when my expectations weren't met or if I felt I had failed something or someone. When this happens it is like a vail of dark fog rolls over me. I feel it all over my body. It makes it very hard to think straight and sometimes nearly impossible to function. The feeling of a weighted blanket or trying to run through loose sand. It is so hard to move and nearly impossible to get anywhere in a hurry.

Every time I had a depressive episode, which in my case could swing so viciously into thoughts of suicide, the overwhelming feeling that I was losing control or approval from that person and that I was going to be left alone with no one was also a common theme.

Now I am very independent and like my personal space and alone time. However when I meet or engage with someone I really click with or feel a deep connection with, I would immediately latch on and sink my codependent teeth right into them. I had no chill.

My mind would build up these stories and idolize these relationships or connections and I would basically build my life around how I needed them. Without them I would not survive and be doomed to walk the planet alone and never be happy or satisfied on my own. These thoughts and emotions are pretty scary. To give all my self worth and power to someone else and to believe that their opinion was more important than my own, would leave me feeling defeated. I needed someone else to validate me in every way because I felt so insecure and unsure about myself and who I was. I was allowing them to control my mind and dictate my emotions.

I can sense I'm going to slide under the fog of depression and I have to act quickly. My down time is not nearly as bad as it used to be. Sometimes I would be incapacitated for days on end. Never leaving my bed. The sun was way too bright and happy to be faced.

"I will because I can. I can because I will."

When I saw this pattern and the weight and value I put on my relationships and I was able to change it. I was able to show myself that I am the person I should be idolizing. I am the queen who deserves to be on that throne because I have taken the time and done the work to learn and take care of myself and my needs first. I am the one I have to come home to and go to bed with every night. If I don't like who I am, what I am doing and what I am thinking, only I can change that and only I will change that. Once I found out who I was and what I wanted, the darkness got a bit lighter. When I reminded myself of all I have done and all I will do, the fog began to lift.

A pep talk with yourself, hold up, let's be honest, a whole pep rally for yourself is necessary. I am the only one that can control my mind. I am the only one who I really believe and can convince at the same damn time. Like I said I still fall under this spell of depression now and again but now I take it as a reminder of how bad ass I am. It's the opportunity to give myself a lifetime achievement award ceremony to let myself know I can do anything.

"YOU'VE HAD THE POWER ALL ALONG MY DEAR."

Glinda ,the Good Witch
Wizard of Oz

Your Own Personal Super Hero

Now that we have addressed the negative thoughts, inner critics and saboteurs that reside in our minds, it's time to address the other side.

Someone who doesn't get nearly enough air time and next to zero credit. I am talking about your alter ego. That part of you that can do anything, think anything and say anything. Everyone has one and it is their time to shine.

As much as you can be a Negative Nancy or Debbie Downer, you also have the capability to be your own super hero and knight in shining armor.

Do you ever notice how easy it is to lean toward the negative. It's because us humans are designed to constantly be on the look out for flaws and risk. We are always on the defense to protect ourselves from being hurt. Even from a very young age when you told your parents you wanted to be an actress or start a band or become a dinosaur. Whatever your hopes and dreams were as a child, you were always encouraged to have a backup plan, a plan B.

This is where your plan B becomes BS. When you turn on your alter ego, anything and I mean anything, can happen. We all have the capability to turn our inner superhero on. We did it non stop as a kid. Make believe and fantasy was our everyday reality, we didn't know any other way.

Creating an alter ego is not just for kids. We see them all the time. From Beyonce, Oprah, Lady Gaga, they all step up and step into characters they have created and personified. Even Martin Luther King had an alter ego. He wore glasses because he thought they made him look more distinguished, not because he needed them. By wearing glasses he felt smarter. Martin Luther King created this alter ego so he could step into the man he needed to be to deliver speeches and allowed him to fight the resistance, that inner voice that tells us we can't, when we absolutely can.

I bet you have created an alter ego of your own and you don't even realize it. Think back to what kind of person you are at home versus who you are at work. Who you are around children as opposed to your girlfriends at book club. We have different versions of ourselves for different situations and that's ok. In fact it is great that we are able to adjust according to our surroundings and audience. I don't know about you, but I sure as heck wouldn't talk to my girlfriends the way I talk to my 2 year old niece and vice versa. My 2 year old niece does not want to hear me cursing about my sex life, or lack thereof.

No matter what age you are, your creative imagination is your greatest superpower. Everyone has an alter ego, but not everyone knows how to unlock this other version of themselves. Your alter ego isn't about being fake, it's about using your imagination to discover the hero inside and overcome negative feelings of self-doubt and insecurity. Your superhero is your saboteurs worst nightmare.

It is time for you to unlock those limiting beliefs that have kept you where you are. By taking control of your mind you are able to change your narrative. Your alter ego is here to help you break those patterns and step into who you truly are.

Our inner critic likes to pop up whenever they see fit. Our Alter ego takes a bit more practice and needs to be amped up and encouraged to come out and play. You can create an alter ego for any situation you need a boost of confidence in.

Steps to Empowering Your Inner Super Hero

1. Context

What situation will you use this particular super hero in. You can build different alter egos for different situations in your life.

Example: You work in sales and want to be a bad ass selling machine. You want to listen to your customers needs and wants, speak with conviction and articulate your sales points with ease.

2. Name your superhero

Come up with a name that is significant and has meaning. You can base it on the name of someone you admire, or the name of your favorite superhero. You can add an adjective to your name like "The Great" or add "2.0 version."

Example: Beyonce uses "Sasha Fierce" to step into her sexuality and power before she hits the stage. David Bowie created "Ziggy Stardust" to become a fearless humanoid alien.

3. Describe your superhero

Who is your alter ego and how do they move through the world? What qualities do they possess that are going to help you achieve your goals once you step inside this character? Describe their personality.

4. Wardrobe

Create a uniform for your super hero. Because this is mainly a mindset change, having something tangible like clothing makes it easier to physically slip into the character of your alter ego. Think of a special pair of pants or a magic scarf. Describe how your super hero dresses.

I used to be so embarrassed and ashamed of my depression. I felt that by admitting I was sad, meant that I wasn't or couldn't be happy, bubbly and bright as well. I didn't understand why I couldn't just be a happy person all the time.

As Dolly Parton says:

"You must endure the rain in order to see the rainbow."

If everything was sunshine and lollipops all the time we would need some heavy duty sunglasses so we weren't blinded by all the sun and we would also need a damn good dentist to deal with all the cavities from all those lollipops!

The Gate Keeper

Debbie tried to control the music.

I had the tendency to listen to slow, super depressing love ballads. Usually about heartbreak and super sad shit. I wasn't even going through a break up but because I was constantly listening to this sad EMO music, it made my subconscious believe that I was! Heaven forbid I listened to my sad girl playlist on a day when I was actually sad, it was over! It was a downward spiral and these sad and excruciating painful love songs made me feel worse. It was like tossing another log in the engine of the train to Sadville! It didn't do anything for me.

When I decided to save myself and change my life, I took note of what I was listening to. Whether it was conversations I was having, the people around me, the music I was listening to, even the tv shows and movies I was watching, they all had the same common theme.

They all seemed to be sad and on the negative side. So you can only imagine the effect hearing, seeing and being involved in all this negativity day in and day out had on me. I was contributing to the negative Nancy and Debbie downer in my mind. It sounds so simple and a no brainer, but pay attention. Listen to the subject of your conversations, are they based on negative experiences? Are you commiserating with your friends over something negative? Do you complain and resort to negative Nancy to find some commonality within your relationships? What music do you listen to ? What TV shows and movies do you watch ?

Mind Your Mind

Your mind is the greatest most intricate computer ever built. Your Mac or PC has a certain amount of storage and then it maxes out. It stops storing and functioning to the best of its ability. Our minds never max out and can never be filled. Our mind is begging for knowledge and memories, so fill it with good shit ! You put good in, you get good out.

Speaking of getting good out, choosing your words wisely is key when communicating with others and especially yourself. Refrain from using the words, "should" and "have to." These words are the kiss of death. They automatically put a negative spin on whatever you are talking about and the goal is to keep yourself in a positive mindset right? So stop using daunting, negative words to describe what you are doing and how you move through your life. We all have choices, we can choose to see the negative side or the positive side of every single situation. We communicate these choices through the words we use to describe our life.

Say you are unhappy with your weight and want to change that. The most common sentence to describe this situation would be "I **have** to lose weight, I **need** to work out and I **should** eat healthier." If you are around a group of women for more than 3.5 seconds, these sentences are pretty common.

How can we change these sentences from pain and despair to having the power and control to make these wishes and desires, and ultimately a choice, a reality? We change the words used to achieve this goal. The word "lose" implies that you want to eventually find what you have lost or you are mourning something that is gone.

Let's replace "lose" with words like release or shed.

As far as using "need to" or "have to," that automatically implies that the task is a chore. If you flip the script and come from a place where you "get to" or "you want to," then it tips the power scale in your favor. You are in control, you are running the show because you are grateful and thankful you have the opportunity to make decisions and save your own damn life. The power and control not only lies in your actions but in your words. You have the power and don't you forget it.

How I tap into self worth and tend to the garden of my mind every day is through affirmations and manifestations. You are your own cheerleader and the authority of your mind. What you allow in, how your thoughts are processed and what you need and deserve, is up to you.

In order to create an affirmation for yourself that is effective you have to believe it. Both sides of your brain need to believe what your saying is true or possible, in order for an affirmation to work.

Our brain is such a magical tool that we essentially have two of them. The left hemisphere that handles the logical, fact based, analytical thinking. And the right which is more creative, imaginative and stores more emotional expression. Each hemisphere can fully function on its own, they are that powerful. In order for an affirmation to really work, a thought must be congruent in each side of the brain. It must register and check off all the boxes in both hemispheres. You must feel, smell, taste, and see your affirmation to fully turn on and engage the whole brain.

If this isn't achieved you will never fully believe or have faith in the thoughts you are feeding your mind. Your goal won't be achieved because you don't believe it can happen or that you're not worthy of it happening to you. The goal is to find the sweet spot. Using our words to find the balance between right and left brain dominance to create a super kick ass fully functioning mind and in turn life.

I have a method to get both sides of your brain on board and create strong affirmations that will allow you to manifest every-thing your heart desires. Follow these Jedi Mind tricks below to create your own personal affirmations to save your own damn life.

Jedi Mind Tricks to Creating Manifestations That Work:

1. Focus

What do you want? What do you want your affirmation to be directed to? You can use these manifestations to attract everything and anything you want in your life. From relationships, career, health, addictions you name it. If you can think it, you can achieve it.

2. Be Present

Now, this is where the logic police step in. I don't mean to be a buzz kill, but telling yourself over and over again that you are rich while living in your mom's basement isn't going to work. It's not that I don't want you to be rich, I do! Trust me I want you to get that money, honey. But feeding yourself incongruent thoughts and words are not going to get you there. Your mind is smarter than that. Your body has a physical reaction to bullshit and will work against you. Neglecting to acknowledge your present reality is the biggest disservice you can do to yourself.

Here are some examples:

" I am rich" to " I am working and learning every day towards a life of infinite prosperity"

"I am healthy" to "I am taking every step to maintain and ensure a healthy lifestyle"

When you acknowledge your present state your affirmations get much more specific. Both sides of the brain can compute and get on board without any hesitation. That's when you know you have a strong affirmation.

57

3. Words

Be mindful of what you say, and even more of what you don't.

Don't wish for things you don't want. Sounds simple right? I always hear people talking about what they don't want. Stay in the positive, your subconscious mind doesn't recognize what you want or not want. By stating what you don't want leaves a blank spot and lack of direction. Therefore the brain doesn't know how to compute.

Here are some examples:

"I don't want to be judge mental" to "I want to be open and accepting of the world around me"

" I don't want to drink anymore" to " I want to make healthy life choices that make me feel good."

* This one really hit home for me. Flipping the switch from what I didn't want to what I wanted for my life made not drinking and sobriety a no-brainer.

4. Have fun

Take time each day to acknowledge what you are grateful for. An attitude of gratitude primes your mind for success!

You are the gatekeeper to your mind. Whatever passes through the gates of your mighty brain must pay a toll. Just like your body, what are you feeding your mind. How are you nourishing and expanding that beautiful bounty of knowledge.

Write your affirmations here:

Commitment No. 3

Connection

"I define connection as the energy that exists between people when they feel seen, heard, and valued; when they can give and receive without judgment; and when they derive sustenance and strength from the relationship." -Brene Brown

Y ou are the sum of the company you keep. Your connections to those around you directly affect and influence
your thoughts, feelings and choices. There is no greater joy than caring for the ones you love. However in order to
survive we don't need other people, We *want* other people. We
want to find others to love us and care for us and for us to be
able to do the same for another human being.

Let me explain why this is a want. In adulthood we have very
little needs. Essentially to survive all we need is the air that we
breathe, food and water. Those three things are essential needs
that every person has in order to survive. If you look at it that
way the rest is just icing on the cake! Contrary to popular belief
you don't need a certain type of sports car in your garage and
you don't need that bag of chips, Carol! But let's get real, they
sure are nice to have. These wants are just that, wants. You are
not going to stop breathing because you don't have them.

The same applies to connections in your life. You don't need
anyone in your life. You can absolutely make your way through
life on your own. Life is much more meaningful when we have
someone that we love to share our experiences with. So how do
you find people you want in your life? How do you choose your
connections wisely? You must first start with the most important connection of all, yourself.

**When you know yourself
you are empowered.
When you accept yourself
you are invincible.**

Tina Lifford

Connection to Yourself

Having a connection with yourself is the longest, most difficult, yet most rewarding relationship you will ever experience. When all the noise and chatter has subsided you are left with only one person, you.

My favorite way to get in touch with myself is to interview myself. Yeah you heard right! Pretend you are in an interview with yourself and answer the following questions. This is a great way to put aside some of those emotions that may inhibit you from answering honestly. By removing your emotions you may be shocked at some of the answers you come up with.

There is no right or wrong answer to the following questions. It's all self exploration baby!

Interview You Questions:

1. Describe your perfect day.

Who are you with, what are you doing, where are you in the world? How does it feel to live out this perfect day? Get as detailed as possible.

Example: Waking up beside someone I love and having coffee in bed with our dogs, a hike up a new trail, a dip in our hot tub to prepare us for our massages. A nice sushi dinner followed by a movie in a theatre with big reclining chairs. I love the whole movie theatre experience, from the chairs to the smell of popcorn to the sound system. A drive home to our house in the woods and a long walk with the dogs before settling into bed.

2. What makes your heart sing ?

When all is said and done, everything on the to do list has been crossed off, what do you do that is just for you? What do you find joy in? Think back to childhood. What were you doing when you were most happy and care free?

Tap into your 5 senses: smell, sight, taste, touch and hearing. Come up with something for each sense. These don't have to be huge, monumental things in your life. Look for the little things that light you up throughout your day.

Example: Watching my dog run through the park, the smell and feel of fresh clean sheets, the sound of my best friend laughing.

3. Where do you see yourself in 5 years?

This is probably one of my favorite questions. I want you to find the balance between fantasy and reality and construct what you want, not what you need for yourself in 5 years. Notice how I said where do you "see" yourself not where are you in five years. I want you to dive into your imagination and think where will you be if you keep your routine up or what will happen if you make a shift and save your own damn life. This question is so open and vague, you can't help but have fun with it!

Topics to write about: relationships, career, environment etc.

Example: I am a bright, fun loving, generous, smart, boss living in a large house with a yard for my dog with beautiful landscaping and a horseshoe driveway. A huge kitchen with two sinks. I am married and travel a lot for work and pleasure. My partner gets to come with me and we make amazing memories together exploring the world. Maybe I retire in a villa somewhere in the jungle of Mexico, who knows!

_____

_____

_____

_____

_____

4. What are you ashamed of?

What is a topic about yourself that you avoid talking about? You can feel shame about anything in your life. You can feel shame for thoughts or actions or even things you can't control. We all deal with varying degrees of shame, this is a chance to acknowledge it. Write it down. Spell it out.

Example: I constantly felt shame for how I treated people. I didn't have any patience or empathy as I moved through the world. I thought that everyone owed me something and why do I always have to suffer. I was ashamed of this behavior.

ARE YOU

Having Fun?

Once you have answered those four questions, what do you see? Any patterns or themes coming up? Take note if it was effortless or painful to answer those questions.

This is an opportunity to try new things. Find out and be mindful of what makes your heart sing or where you want to see yourself in five years. You don't have to know all the answers right now, that is part of the fun.

Keep these questions in the back of your mind as you make your way through your day and through this book. Be mindful of what your days consist of and how it makes you feel.

Now that you know what you like and a bit more about yourself, its time to implement more of these things into your daily routine. Just like you have to plan for success, you have to plan for happiness and this starts with you and connecting to what brings you joy.

Connection to yourself isn't just about finding things you like and don't like. It's about finding that truth, that sweet spot when you are unapologetically yourself. You are willing to deal with the ramifications and backlash you are going to get from being your full self. That is connection to yourself. This level of connection is not only extremely empowering it contains a type of energy that is so magnetic and makes people gravitate towards you because they feel safe. They feel safe because you are so sure of yourself it exudes confidence.

This conviction to your connection with yourself, your beliefs and values puts others in a trance, in the best possible way!

Journey back to when you were young and had that innocent sense of not giving a fuck about who said what and why. We all had that sense of freedom and innate self assurance when we were children. However, time and society took its toll on us and we learned to doubt ourselves. We learned to give our power away and in turn our connection to ourself got numb or was even lost. It's like only having one bar on your wifi signal. It is there but nothing is getting through.

Don't worry all hope is not lost. Disconnection from yourself is a learned behavior, a defense mechanism if you will. Society has taught us to conform and constrict ourselves in order to survive. And by survive I mean fit in and be accepted to avoid pain and suffering. Because we learned these behaviors we can easily unlearn them or re learn how to be our true selves. Enough with the blame game and society this and society that. We have the power to revert back to our child like days when our connection to ourselves was all we needed.

The Shame Game

I didn't even realize how compromised my connection had been. I never took the time to realize why it was such a challenge for me to be social and meet new people. Self deprecation was always a topic of choice when I was lost for words and I never understood why I felt such comfort from beating myself up or joking about myself to my own dismay.

It all clicked one day when I was working through a manifesting course. The first question in the second part of the course was " What in your life are you ashamed of?"" What is a topic about yourself that you avoid talking about?" When I thought back to being out in bars, meeting people for the first time, or just socializing in general, it hit me like a ton of bricks. I was so unbelievably ashamed and embarrassed that I was a gay woman. I hated that part of myself so much, I didn't want to acknowledge it existed. I developed some unhealthy ways of ignoring it. I had so much shame around my sexuality because to me it meant failure. I felt that I was less than any straight or heterosexual person.

Relationships are such a large part of my life and I put so much value on them, I didn't realize that the shame was buried so deep and masked itself with so many layers. I had no idea I was ashamed of my sexual orientation and that it was a huge blockage in connecting with others both personally and especially professionally. I was way too scared to bring it up, I would crack a joke about me being a lesbian before anyone else got a chance at it. What I didn't realize was by burring that shame and disrespecting myself, I allowed others to disrespect me as well. The self deprecation around my sexuality was just a front for the pain and hurt I was in because I was so ashamed to be myself.

Being a gay woman for me was nothing but negative. It was a strike against me because I categorized my sexuality as less than. I defined lesbians as unattractive, unsuccessful, and unintelligent species. By associating or admitting that I was a lesbian meant that I was all of those negative qualities. This is how I thought of myself.

Having such a strong lack of connection to my sexuality and who I was as a person hindered my relationships and connections to others in ways I never realized. I was not honest. I was lying to myself and to others. I had no validity in anything I said because I was talking out two sides of my mouth. I didn't have my own back so how in the hell could I have anyone else's? I felt that if I diluted my gayness it would be easier for people to digest. In fact it was quite the opposite. People didn't know if I was coming or going. I will tell you one thing, conviction and sticking to your guns is sexy as hell! I said it before and I will say it again commitment is sexy and commitment to yourself is "muy caliente!" (That means very hot in Spanish!)

This was a major blockage in connecting to myself. The good thing about this is that these were all just thoughts. They were not facts. How I connected to myself was by finding the facts. I set out to prove myself wrong and that I was in fact none of those things. I did this by finding expanders. Expanders are people that you can relate to. They possess something you want, or have some type of commonality. In my case I set out to find expanders to bust my myth that lesbians were low on the totem pole. I found expanders that were similar to me in age, who were successful, attractive, pretty damn smart and articulate!

By finding positive role models as expanders I proved my negative thoughts wrong. I now had facts and living proof that my negative connection to my sexuality was my perception and not the truth. Much like we did in writing manifestations, by finding and listing these expanders and examples of positive role models that possessed qualities and similarities to myself, I was able to get both sides of my brain on board and form a strong connection to my self. Because my thoughts were congruent about my new found feelings, I was able to forge a stronger connection to myself.

Accepting yourself for who you are is a beautiful fucking thing! It is so exhilarating and liberating to live in self acceptance. True connection with yourself is when you can be honest about all aspects of your character and what makes you, you. Be honest with yourself and love your way through it. If that isn't self love, I don't know what is!

List things you love about yourself:

"Because the greatest

Love of all is happening to me.

I found the greatest

Love of all inside of me!"

Whitney Houston

Check Yourself Before You Wreck Yourself

The funniest thing happened when I started building a strong connection to myself. I stopped talking shit. I stopped the petty, mindless gossip that happens in circles of people that are too scared to connect with themselves. I became too damn connected and solid with myself that talking about people or even thinking about people in a negative way didn't work with my new found higher level of thinking. I am thinking bigger. I am now in it for the long haul and my feelings, my actions and my words all support that.

Today we have many forms of disconnection that are masked and packaged as tools for building connections. They are just distractions. They are "fuck it" buttons. You push these buttons when you want to disengage and disconnect.

Technology is a great example. Computers and the internet have allowed us to fully disconnect and disengage from ourselves and others. Everything is so convenient. It is much easier to be distracted by something on TV or Facebook then it is to look inward and find out who you are.

The moment of so called "peace" or relaxation you supposedly get from watching Youtube, scrolling through Instagram or having a glass of wine is all just temporary. How can we possibly find peace or practice self care when we don't really know anything about ourselves. How can you know how to treat and heal yourself if you are constantly hitting the "fuck it" button to distract and alter your mental state? To even attempt to take care of someone you need to know the person you are caring for and their needs. Guess what honey, the patient is you!

The real peace comes from being one with yourself and loving yourself. Do the work, find out who you are, what you like and learn how to love her. You may not always like yourself, but having love and understanding for yourself, makes life so much easier and definitely more enjoyable. Last time I checked you can't hate yourself into loving yourself.

Figuring out my love language gave me insight to how I needed to feel loved and how to harness my relationships and show up for my friends and loved ones. Wouldn't it just be so much easier if we could just learn how to harness our love for ourselves and for others? At the end of the day we all want to feel loved and that has different meaning and feeling for everyone.

IF YOU CAN'T LOVE YOURSELF, HOW THE HELL YOU GONNA LOVE SOMEBODY ELSE?

Ru Paul

Seeing as we can only be responsible for ourselves, getting to know how you interpret love is a must. By learning your love language you will be armed with the knowledge of what you need in a relationship from a spouse, business partner, friends, family members etc. By knowing what makes you feel loved and appreciated you can in turn teach others how you want to be treated.

The Five Love Languages by Gary Chapman, describe the ways we feel loved and appreciated. Depending on our individual personality types, you may feel loved differently than how your partner does. Your love language is valid in all relationships, not just romantic partners. Understanding and decoding these love languages will help you determine and understand where others stand but most importantly how you feel loved and what you need from your relationships.

The most common issue people have is the lack of connection. That lack of connection to self and the people around them makes them feel isolated, misunderstood and alone. By learning your love language and your loved ones love language, you will have a head start to building a solid foundation and connection.

The 5 Love Languages

Love Language #1: Words of Affirmation

This love language expresses love with words that build your partner up. Verbal compliments don't have to be complicated; the shortest and simplest words of affirmation can be the most effective.

"You always make me laugh."

"I love your hair today."

Words mean a lot to a person with this love language. Compliments and an "I love you" can go a long way. On the other side, negative or insulting comments can hurt this person and take longer to forgive than others.

Love Language #2: Acts of Service

Your partner might have this love language if their motto is "Actions speak louder than words."

This love language expresses itself by doing things that you know your spouse would like. Cooking a meal, doing the laundry, and picking up a prescription, are all acts of service. They require some thought, time, and effort.

All of these things must be done with positivity and with your partner's ultimate happiness in mind to be considered an expression of love. Actions out of obligation and with a negative tone are something else entirely.

Love Language #3: Receiving Gifts

No, this love language isn't necessarily materialistic. It just means that a meaningful or thoughtful gift makes them feel appreciated and loved. Something as simple as picking up a pint of their favorite ice cream after a long work week can make an impact on this love language.

This is different than Acts of Service – those are purely helpful and taking work off of your partner's plate.

Love Language #4: Quality Time

This love language is all about undivided attention. No televisions, no phones, or any other distractions. They think talk is cheap and the type of action they want is to be your main focus.

This means that you need to make sure to dedicate time together to create experiences together. That will help them feel comforted in the relationship.

Every time you cancel a date, postpone time together or aren't present during your time together, it can be hurtful to your partner.

Love Language #5: Physical Touch

To this love language, nothing is more impactful than the physical touch of their partner. They aren't necessarily into over-the-top PDA, but they do feel more connected and safe in a relationship by holding hands, kissing, hugging, etc.

If physical touch is a person's primary love language, without it they will feel unloved. All of the words and gifts in the world won't change that.

Circle in this book your love language. Most people have a combination of a few. Try and really weed out your strongest and which one you react to the most.

My love language is #3 Receiving Gifts. I fought and resisted it because I thought it meant I was a horrible shallow person. I mean I do live in LA, did the shallowness rub off on me? I took this a step further and really thought back to what gifts stood out and what they meant to me. The gifts that really stood out and made me feel loved were an extension of me. They were thoughtful small gifts that only someone who really listened and understood who I was would know to get me.

What gifts symbolize to me is strong, deep connection. That someone was listening and paying attention to me, and I felt heard and appreciated. If someone gave me a gift I loved, it was a good sign because they knew me and listened to me. The real me. I can pin point exactly how connected and where the relationship is going by the gifts. The superficial relationships when my so called partner didn't make the effort to know me, listen to me or even really care to, was reflected in their gift giving. Truth be told I have received a lot of horrible gifts. Not once but twice I got one of those hoover board scooters. I am a thirty something woman, who can barely balance on a two wheel bike and you are giving me an LED light up balancing hoover board? Definitely not my jam.

When your love language is gifts you have basically materialized your gauge for connection. Underneath that wrapping paper is a visual representation of your relationship to that person. It's terrifying and extremely disappointing when it doesn't all line up.

Nothing says, "I don't listen to you or understand anything about you," like a pair of Crocs for a girl who lives and dies for nothing but heels.

By understanding how you feel loved, appreciated and heard, you will be able to communicate that in your relationships. If you continue to not feel appreciated this is a good sign that this isn't the relationship for you and if you aren't getting what you need from the relationship, its time to move on.

Connection with Others

A connection with someone else can either light you up with energy or suck the life out of you and drag you down to dullsville. Not everyone is going to be for you and that's ok, that is part of finding your tribe. It is essential to release the life suckers in order to make room for the energy sources. Occupying your time with people who aren't fulfilling your needs and wants is very draining. You can't do fun shit with people who aren't fun! Being in a bad relationship is like a ball trying to through itself. It's super frustrating and you get nowhere fast.

There is nothing that will distract you, annoy you, frustrate you or demoralize you quicker than a shitty relationship. FYI: This is not limited to romantic relationships. I'm talking about anyone you come in contact with, and any unresolved issues, resentment and frustration with any human being in your life. Mom, Dad, brother, sister, coworker, ex partner, spouse, kids, everyone and anyone. It starts with you.

"Resentment is like taking poison and expecting the other person to die."

Poor relationships will occupy and control your mind. Here's the kicker. You're in control, you get to decide if you drink the poison or not. The only one who can make that choice is you. Relationships and connections have a direct and serious impact on your mental and physical health. Ever had a break up or dealt with family drama so exhausting that you can't muster up enough energy to go to work or follow through with other commitments?

When you have poor relationships it causes you to be distracted and not run at 100%. If your distracted and allowing your energy to be sucked by un fulfilling relationships you are taking energy away from the good ones. Let's say your co worker is pissing you off. This drama and this bullshit takes a percentage of your daily capacity. Let's say 30% is no longer dedicated to the good stuff in your mind. So now you only have 70% of all that power, clarity, peace and love. See graph for details:

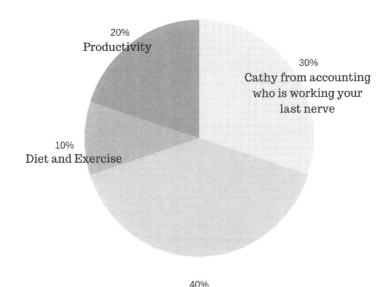

Now that's just one person, one situation, how many other people do you give a piece of your happiness to?

Maybe you have someone you have unresolved issues with.

Maybe your parents weren't there for you as a kid.

Maybe a friend betrayed your trust.

Maybe your partner broke your heart into a million pieces.

I get it. I have been there. It happens to all of us.

However, at the end of the day, how you choose to deal with it and the baggage you carry from those relationships is up to you. You are single handedly giving away your power, energy and peace of mind. That's right. You are to blame. Now I know what your thinking, but they did this to me and they made me act like that. They made me act crazy! Girl, if I had a dollar for every time I heard someone say that, I would be a multi millionaire.

Understand this. If there is any drama, resentment, bitterness, or anger in your life its 100% your responsibility. You and you alone are making the conscious choice to stay in that state, regardless of what the other person has done to you. You can not force your neighbor to trim their over grown hedges, that's on them.

Thinking you can change them by force or guilt, is like giving away a piece of your mind. Every single time you allow an unresolved issue to remain in your space, it's just draining your energy. Energy you could use to build solid relationships with people you actually like.

Bitterness and resentment clutters your mind and steals your happiness. You need to harness and protect your energy. Be picky with who you spend your time and energy with.

As an adult my relationship with my Mom has been strained. I have been angry with her for many years. I was angry and frustrated and didn't agree with choices she had made. I was mad at her for not being assertive and standing up for herself and I felt like I needed to protect her and save her. Then it hit me, I had this realization.

She didn't know any better. She was doing the best she could to survive.

Being mad at my Mom and treating my Mom with such disrespect doesn't help me. Treating her poorly doesn't make me feel good. It doesn't change the past or secure the future. It doesn't create anything good within our relationship. If anything my resentments towards her drives us further and further away from achieving the relationship I really want. It doesn't make me more successful in my business, it doesn't make me a better partner or daughter and it certainly doesn't help me get a 6 pack at the gym! What positive things are happening to me in my life because I am holding on to hate and resentment towards my Mom? What good is holding onto that anger doing for me ?

Absolutely nothing. Holding onto that anger and hurt was not serving me at all. Holding onto all that negative energy creates and breeds negativity. I hit my limit. My energy was maxed out. I crossed my threshold and no longer tolerated a shitty relationship with my Mom. I was so hurt. I thought by hurting her I would teach her a lesson or give her a taste of her own medicine.

I was done. I had no other option but to face this anger and hurt head on and to reach out. I picked up the phone and called my Mom. Our relationship wasn't horrible but it also wasn't great. Our conversations would center around surface type things like shopping and home decor. Nothing anything deeper than that. I wanted more. I wanted to have a deeper connection with my Mom and I had to bring up, work through and heal the past in order to better the future.

We both agreed we needed to work some stuff out and committed to going to therapy together. Together we confronted our drama, beef, resentments, unresolved issues whatever you want to call it. We aired our shit out and got down to work. It was hard. It was scary and was very uncomfortable at times. But being vulnerable will heal you. Regardless of the other persons reaction, being vulnerable and speaking your truth will set you free.

I love my Mom, I truly do, but I love myself even more. I mended my strained relationship with my Mom for me. Because at the end of the day I want to feel better. I want to feel better about myself and eliminate any relationship that is weighing me down. I was sick and tired of my head being consumed with negativity and being set off by every little thing or comment my Mom or anyone else made.

When I confronted and repaired my relationship with my Mom, I set the bar for all my other relationships. This strained relationship took up a huge amount of emotional real estate, more than I could afford. Once I freed up this real estate is when I had room to grow and cultivate relationships I wanted in my life. The way I see it is life isn't too short to hold grudges or have bad blood with anyone. It's quite the opposite.

Life is too damn long. Life is too long to continue to entertain straining, energy sucking, drama filled relationships. Those negative connections are what will cut your life short. Life is too long, so cut the bullshit. Reach out to those you miss and those you want to repair a relationship with. Not for their sake, but for your own mental health. To keep your side of the street clean. All the other relationships that have done you wrong, release them. Instead of a "fuck you," send them off with an "I appreciate you." Listen, you and only you, are in control of who you talk to, who you work with, who you sleep with, and who you go to dinner with.

You are 100% in control of the other humans you allow into your space every day. If there is contention or unresolved issues, it's up to you to fix them or release them. It's your choice to yell and curse out some crazy driver and it's your choice to stay mad at someone no matter what they have done. Now, you can't change how other people act. Assholes will be just that, assholes. What you can change is how you interact with them. Choosing whether or not you're going to allow them to take up mental real estate in your head.

If you had $86,400 and someone stole $10, would you throw $86,390 away for revenge? Or move on and live? Right, move on and live. See, you have 86,400 seconds each day. Don't let someone's negative 10 seconds ruin the remaining 86,390. Life is bigger than that. And so are you.

Creating boundaries in a relationship is the most important and difficult thing to do. Trust me, I have been through it with my Mom. I can't change her. I am only responsible for myself, my actions, my thoughts and my energy.

Keeping your relationships in check is difficult but it needs to be done if you want to have peace, clarity and success.

Our greatest achievements are gained from being vulnerable. Public speaking is an example of being vulnerable. You must be open and honest and vulnerable to deliver a successful speech that people can relate to. In being vulnerable you build peoples trust and let them see the real you. What you get in return are all the feels. A rush of adrenaline a sprinkle of endorphins and a mound of deep meaningful connections.

This is a feeling we want every damn day. But when we are walking around with all these blockages and our emotional real estate tied up in relationships that are sucking the life out of us, it is nearly impossible to be vulnerable.

For years I thought I loved drinking. Don't get me wrong I liked the taste of champagne and some wine just fine, but what I liked more was what drinking represented. I wanted the connection that drinking seemed to facilitate. I liked going out and being with friends and meeting new people. Turns out drinking was just the unhealthy, toxic glue holding my so called connections together.

Trying to build solid connections with people while drinking is basically like wiping your ass with a hoop. Nothing is real. Alcohol actually prohibits us from making soulful, sustainable and genuine connections. You are in an altered state. Remember, I thought I needed to be the girl dancing on tables, flipping my hair back and forth to be interesting enough for people to want to talk to me. Lies, all lies!

Don't even get me started on dating. I believed whole heartedly that I couldn't meet someone new without having a drink in hand, or at least be a couple drinks deep. I needed that courage, which turns out was disconnection from myself. That disconnection allowed me to shut off my senses, specifically my common sense. My drunken state would allow me to bypass my natural shy, introvert, stand in the corner and don't make eye contact with anyone, behavior and slip into arrogant, life of the party asshole. Which I mistakingly confused and sold to my victims, I mean partners, as confidence.

Every relationship I started and maintained this way has failed. Miserably. Not being my authentic self in a relationship, of any kind, eventually ran it's course and ended up becoming a huge dumpster fire. When there is a disconnection from yourself, the people and the purpose of that relationship, that my friend, is a recipe for a perfect shit storm.

When you have a true, genuine connection with someone it almost feels like you have known them before or in a past life. It's easy and your conversations flow. There is a give and take and an unwritten understanding. You feel energized and inspired and full of life when you are around these people. You feel heard, understood and acknowledged. Congratulations! This is the sign of a strong connection. This is how you should feel around the people you choose to spend your time with. Keep this energy going, cultivate relationships with these people.

Where do you find these kick ass, rainbow, fairy, mermaid like connections? You find them in the things you like to do. You cultivate these friendships in the activities that light you up. Coming together to celebrate something, anything, is a great foundation to build a connection with someone. Think about that hip hop dance class you love. The music and the energy of the room gets you excited and pumped up! Not only are you working out and sweating, you are enjoying yourself and having fun. You then meet another person who feels the same way about the class and boom you have these strong feelings and emotions in common and you have something to celebrate. Chances are if you like the same dance class you will have other things in common and will strengthen your bond even further.

When you come together to celebrate you are keeping the positive energy flowing. It is so much easier to have a strong connection with someone based on something positive than negative. It is so much lighter, and much more fulfilling to talk about things we like. Our hopes and dreams of taking over the world, sharing passions and what is going right in our lives. To sit there and gossip about other people and listen to your friend talk about how tired, bored and broke she is because she refuses to dump her money sucking leach of a boyfriend, is no bueno. Pity parties are not fun to attend.

See the difference? Even the negative words are hard to read. Stay in the positive, go towards the light ! Life is too long to be bogged down by energy vampires and strained connections that leave you feeling exhausted from trying to make it work. It should flow. It should be easy and it should be fun. Life is too long to just be tolerating people. I for one don't have the energy to tolerate anyone or anything in my life that doesn't make me feel good. My life is too long, I have too much life to live to be struggling and not enjoying myself.

Remember you are doing this for you, for your health for your well being. The name of the game here is to have strong, healthy relationships with the people in your life, not half ass dramatic ones chock full of resentment.

If there is a significant relationship in your life, invest in that relationship everyday. Talk is cheap actions are gold.

No relationship is too far gone to invest in because you aren't too far gone. Having a great relationship with your lover is liberating. Eliminating contention with family, friends, co workers, is powerful. Free up the mental real estate that drains you and be ready and available for what fuels you and sets your life on fire with love and joy.

As long as there is air in your lungs, you can be adding value to loved ones, showing support and appreciation and creating the exact relationships you want in your life. The number one reason to commit to healthy relationships is for the power and strength you receive. Being of service is the gift that keeps on giving.

The number one mistake people make when trying to form relationships and build connections is being in their own head and consumed by thoughts of being enough.

Most people are too busy being interesting, they forget to be interested.

Step outside yourself. Ask questions and stay curious. What we crave most are deep meaningful connections. In order to establish a deep meaningful conversation, vulnerability is key. We crave it, we want it, we need it, yet it's the thing we are most afraid of. For most people being vulnerable and letting their guard down is a risk and they would be 100% right. But what else is there?

You must invest. Take the time. Make some changes. Be vulnerable if you want to make new connections or mend old ones. There is infinite power available to you when you surround yourself with strong relationships.

Choose to create and harness them by investing in them daily.

Connection to Something Bigger

Connection with something greater than yourself is very powerful. To have faith and trust that there is something within our universe that is more powerful than us takes so much pressure off our backs. To know that the world doesn't revolve around you and that you are not the end all be all is quite comforting.

I thought that I had control and power over every single thing in my life. I inflicted a lot of hurt and pain upon myself thinking that everything revolved around me.

I was always told be careful what I wished for or what I said could come true.

I remember what I said to my Dad like it was yesterday. One night we were watching tv, all the lights were out and just the glare from the screen lit up the room. My Dad sat on the couch and I sat on the floor on my stomach in front of the tv. We were watching our favorite show, Melrose Place. We watched it every single week. Not sure how appropriate it was for a 10 year old to be watching, but that's neither here nor there.

It was the night before my youngest brother Bobby was going to go back into the hospital. He had been battling a form of cancer called retinoblastoma. At this point he had already lost one eye and he was going through chemo and radiation to save the other. The next day was his appointment to see if the treatment was successful. To see if Bobby would be able to continue life with one eye or if he would need to remove his other eye and be blind.

At the commercial break there was an advertisement that mentioned a blind man. I turned to my Dad and asked what would happen if Bobby went blind. I will never forget the look on my Dads face. He looked at me so sternly and his eyes were so sharp. It was as if I had cast a spell or a curse on my brother just by uttering those words. My Dad quickly scolded and shot back at me "why would you ever say that." His face was wrinkled and tense yet his eyes were welling up with tears. He was distraught and scared. Scared because me asking that very question made it real. That there was a good possibility my brother would and could be blind.

That conversation haunted me for more years of my life than I care to admit. Bobby's cancer ended up spreading to his other eye. He had to have his eye removed, leaving him blind for the rest of his life at age 5. I can't begin to tell you how guilty I felt. That by asking or vocalizing the possibility of Bobby going blind I felt responsible.

The 10 year old me thought for years and years that I put a curse on him. I would wonder what would have happened if I never asked my Dad that night while watching Melrose Place, if things would have turned out differently. I was so scared of my own thoughts and words that I shut down and shut off. I truly thought I was so powerful that anything I said or thought, would become reality. This power that I thought I possessed was a burden. It was so much pressure and stress, I was in my head all the time, never in the moment. Worrying constantly that everything was up to me. My very thoughts would become reality.

IT'S ALL CONNECTED.
YOUR GIFTS, YOUR
CIRCUMSTANCE, YOUR
PURPOSE, YOUR
IMPERFECTIONS, YOUR
JOURNEY, YOUR DESTINY.
IT'S MOLDING YOU,
EMBRACE IT.

This so called theory 10 year old me made up, couldn't be further from the truth. The fact of the matter is I had no connection or awareness of anything bigger than myself. You can't blame a 10 year old for thinking that way, but I can when my 10 year old point of view doesn't change when you are pushing thirty. I never grew up or expanded my connection to anything greater than myself. I carried around this guilt and stress thinking that I was to blame and I was responsible.

It wasn't until I began to do the work on myself and discover my real power of surrendering and letting go. If I was as powerful as I had claimed to be all these years, why couldn't I undo or wish for my brothers sight to return or better yet not be struck by cancer in the first place. If I was so powerful why didn't I bring in all the good, all my hopes and dreams, and all the ill will and payback I wanted to inflict on the bullies at school ?

It's because there is something greater than me, than you, than all of us. To quote Gabby Bernstein, " the universe has your back." No matter how tragic things play out they all really do happen for a reason. Things are happening for you, not to you and once you realize that and surrender to the ebb and flow of life, shit gets a whole lot lighter.

You can't control things, people, situations so do yourself a favor and stop trying. Stop worrying and guilt tripping yourself into thinking you have this power, you don't. The only power you have is that in which to govern yourself. Take responsibility for you and you alone.

Everything works together and comes full circle. You can't have one without the other. That being said in order to have these strong connections to your friends, family, partners, co workers, higher power, you name it, you have to be connected to yourself. You have to ground down and really get to know yourself and how you operate and how you want to be in this moment in order to connect fully and whole heartedly with the world around you.

Commitment No.4

Productivity

"The secret of getting ahead is getting started"
-Mark Twain

I t's going to be rough. Point blank, hands down no doubt about it. Doing something new is uncomfortable, it should be. It's new, you haven't done it or been in this situation before. If you feel uncomfortable you are doing it right. The first podcast you record, the first meeting you go to, the first video you produce, your first game. It will all be hard. But you can't make it to your fiftieth without your first.

This is productivity and progression in a nut shell. It's going to suck, it's going to be weird, but you have to just start. You have to get the ball rolling for even a chance at being familiar with something.

What if in six
months from now,
your life was exactly
the same. Are
you ok with that?

That is a hard no, from me. I want to expand. I want to learn more, give more, travel more. I am always progressing and adapting. Now this is not to say that I don't appreciate and are grateful for what I have right now. That is not the case. In fact the exact opposite. I am so grateful and appreciate everything I have and how far I have come that I will attract more.

Moving forward and expanding is the name of the game. If you have too much idle time or become stagnant or some may call it comfortable, that tends to breed contempt. If we aren't moving forward we are moving backwards. This is true as a society and as an individual.

Productivity means different things to different people. In this final commitment to saving your own damn life, I want you to commit to your productivity in all aspects of your life. That means moving forward in all your goals, personally, professionally, spiritually and physically.

Think of yourself as an entrepreneur and you are your business. Your self development is your job. This job will do more than just pay your bills. The return of investment is endless. You have everything to do and little to no accountability. This can be both a blessing and a curse. There is a fine line between being busy and productive. Everyone I know is busy in this day in age, yet no one is getting where they want to be. It seems that if you aren't busy, you aren't living. You don't have to be busy to be important.

I like to read articles that have titles such as "5 Common Traits Among Successful People." I am constantly looking for ways and

Comparing yourself to others isn't productive for personal growth.

commonalities to lump myself into that category. According to one of the articles, all successful people wake up early in the morning and go to bed fairly early each and every day. So of course I thought the only way I was going to be successful and productive was if I woke up early, say 5:30 am and went to bed at 9 pm. I was comparing myself to business dudes who were up in their office plugging away or on their jets to meetings in different cities. Well last time I checked I am not a dude, nor am I in the corporate business world and I definitely don't have a jet, yet.

I also realized that the homeless man that lives in my neighbors carport holds the same hours as the business dudes and look where that got him. If you want to be productive, stop comparing yourself to anyone else. What they are up to or how they got successful is none of your business. There is no secret sauce to being productive and successful in life. You just have to start.

Take what you have learned from the previous chapters and apply it here. Right here and now. Everything you have written down for how you will treat your body, mind and connections, this is where you keep tabs on your business, the business of yourself. Be your own passion project.

Want to feel happy and fulfilled in your life? Get productive. I measure my productivity on a few things. The main thing I used to base my productivity and worth on was money and how much I was making. I never took the time to check in with myself and see if I actually enjoyed what I was doing.

Take my dj career for example. No matter what gig I was doing, what mansion or resort I was traveling to, it was never enough. Full disclosure I was a total grandma princess dj. I would mainly do early evening gigs where the latest I would dj would be 11pm. The longest I ever dj' ed was 4 hours. The numbers seemed pretty easy on paper. However what was hindering my productivity was how drained I would be after every gig. A four hour gig would take me almost a whole day to recover from energetically. Also keep in mind I am sober, so it's not like I had a hangover to nurse, my soul was being absolutely drained by a career I was only in for the paycheck.

When you are just going through the motions for a pay check your productivity hits a ceiling and is at a stand still. Without passion behind what you are doing, this can be a job, being of service, building your own career, if you are just chasing the money you will never be productive, you will just be busy.

Being productive every single day is the backbone to making moves in your life. If you put one foot in front of the other you will move forward, no matter how slow you move the direction is still forward. I am by no means saying that you have to make big moves, hustle every day, bend over backwards to be productive. That's not the way the world works. It's the little steps. The small seemingly insignificant parts of the puzzle that need to be done in order to move forward.

I always told my Mom that I am going to be rich and have a huge house. We would drive by the big fancy houses in Beverly Hills that had two driveways, one for the homeowner and the other a service entrance. I want to be two driveways kind of rich! With a freshly manicured lawn and boxwood hedges shaped to perfection, not one leaf out of place. These big fancy houses always looked so clean and pristine. I would lean over to my Mom and announce " I will own one of those. I am going to be Oprah rich!"

For years I told her this, I drew out what my house would look like and where it would be, the shape of my boxwood hedges and how many would line the driveway. Every single little detail about the house. However one minor, yet major piece of this whole equation was missing. The productivity I was doing in order to make that dream a reality. The steps I was and wasn't taking to making my dream of being a double driveway type of homeowner actually happen.

I had to get real. I had to get honest with myself. This isn't to burst anyones bubble, I love to dream. I am a day dream believer. However I got sick and tired of the talk. Sick and tired of saying one day this, one day that. My reality and day to day productivity was getting me absolutely nowhere close to my dreams. I just kept getting frustrated and discouraged. I became bitter, hard and constantly compared myself to others who had the success that I wanted. I would "yah but" myself to death to make myself feel better about my shortcomings or lack of productivity. If I saw someone with a new car I wanted or career I wanted I would "yah, but her husband paid for it." Or " yah, but her family has all the connections."

Your Future is Hidden in Your Daily Habits.

On social media, all you see is everyone's glow ups, their highlight reel if you will. You don't

Start by drinking a cup of water

Start by paying toward 1 debt

Start by reading 1 page

Start by making 1 sale

Start by deleting 1 old contact

Start by walking 1 lap

Start by attending 1 event

Start by writing 1 paragraph

Start today

know or hear about the hard work or how they prepared themselves to be in that position to reap that type of success. All you are seeing is the 0-100. The truth is most people are primed and plan their success. They don't get picked out of an audience and thrown into fame and fortune. There is training and groundwork laid in order to get to that point.

Look at Justin Bieber, yes he was super young when he was discovered by Usher. However he put in the leg work. He took singing lessons, he took the time to make videos of him singing. He knew what he wanted and he was productive and got himself out there. He was consistent. Justin had goals and wanted to be in the music industry and he made it a priority to record and hone his craft whenever and wherever possible. That is great productivity.

Now I am not saying that you want to be the next Justin Bieber, but do you see where I am going with the steps needed in order to get your pay off. Everyday your productivity must be pushing you forward.

As I kept talking all this talk about a big house, my productivity wasn't walking the walk. I didn't even have credit. I paid for everything in cash. No credit cards, no loans, I was non existent to banks and lenders. That's a bad place to be when you have these big goals and dream of having a mortgage on a mansion. It just doesn't add up. So first things first. I made baby steps toward my goal. I started off with a secured credit card. Then moved on to two credit cards. Then moved on to an auto loan. In a year or so I had built up some decent credit.

I took that a step further. For two years straight I paid off all my credit cards on time and in full every single month. It was like a game for me. I keep at it every single month because I have the bigger picture in the back of my mind. That huge house with a yard and pool, two driveways and boxwood hedges, that is not just a dream. I am closer every day because of small steps I have taken to compound my productivity towards my goal of being a homeowner.

We all know that analogy "how do you eat an elephant? One bite at a time." First off, why in the hell would you want to eat an elephant, and secondly wouldn't you get sick of eating the same thing? If you view the elephant as one giant goal that your whole life depends on, you're setting yourself up for disappointment. So instead of focusing on the end result or finishing the elephant, why not enjoy the bites along the way? Turn your attention to the small victories.

Many people make a major mistake in being entirely focused on big goals. If your goal is to become a best-selling novelist, great. If you base too much of your life satisfaction on achieving it, you'll be unhappy for a very long time quite possibly your whole life.

Long term goals are great, because aiming high lets us strive to be the best we can be. But for every long term goal you have, you want to have many short and medium term goals. If being a best-selling novelist is your long term goal, what smaller goals can you come up with that you need to achieve along the way?

When you have small goals, there are a couple of advantages. First, a small goal gives you something concrete to focus on. If you want to become a best-selling novelist, how will you make that happen?

You can easily be overwhelmed by such a huge task. If you don't know specifically what to do, you're only going to get frustrated. As time goes by, you notice over and over that your goal still hasn't been achieved. It's a heck of a lot easier to come up with a genre or an outline of a book first as a micro goal. Every goal can be broken down into smaller actions and steps. When you outline the steps to do, you're much more likely to get inspired and take action. When you take action you are being productive and moving toward your end game.

Second, you enjoy the satisfaction of achieving a goal and enjoying the benefits. Even if it's a small goal, you feel good for checking it off your to-do list. You also get to have something that brings you a little satisfaction right now. In a world where we are all about the instant gratification, having smaller goals can simulate that and keep you engaged.

Goal Map

Use the spaces to map out steps you need to take to achieve your goal.

_____

                        _____

_____

                        _____

_____

                        _____

_____

Productivity is so much more than how much money you make or the things you acquire to show off how "productive" you are. True productivity is expanding and moving toward something greater than yourself. It's about working within your purpose. It's doing something that lights you up and gets you excited. This can be caring for your family, taking care of loved ones, volunteering for an organization you feel aligned with, working within a field you are proud to be a part of. When you chose to come from passion and from the heart you will be successful by default.

You don't need outside praise or recognition or monetary compensation because you have already won. The thing about productivity is that it breeds achievement. Achieving something in your life brings happiness and joy and a sense of pride. When you are productive and achieve your goals it makes you feel good, and isn't that the point of life to feel good?! When you achieve that diploma from school or get that promotion you have been working toward or send your kids off to college or wake up on time, you have accomplished something.

Since I mentioned the M word, money, I do believe money is a very important piece of the productivity puzzle. It is not the end goal here however, it does help the pieces fit into place. The cold hard truth is that money is needed in our society. It lends us a sense of freedom. Money definitely does not buy happiness but it can ease your mind and allow you some peace. I can't think of anything more taxing or stressful than struggling to make ends meet. Suffering and being in a state of survival is no way to live. When your basic needs are not being met it is pretty hard to think of anything else, let alone dream.

It is impossible to dream big or even imagine larger than life situations when you are struggling to keep a roof over your head and food on the table. Studies show that the high levels of the hormone cortisol, which are produced during periods of stress, may affect the neurotransmitter serotonin and contribute to depression. Fun fact, the main cause of stress and which leads to depression is being in poor financial situations.

Money is freedom. I agree with that because being broke its extremely limiting. The simple fact is, without adequate financial resources you are extremely limited in life. It doesn't mean you can't be happy. But without having money you cannot have the freedom to live life to its full potential. You deserve the best. Point blank. You should not have to struggle to get where you want to be. There is enough freedom pie for everyone to have a slice, hell maybe even two!

Researchers have found that above a certain point, more money does not bring more happiness. Peoples levels of happiness only increase as income increases up to a point. This number is probably smaller than you think, although it depends on where you live, it is usually between $60,000 and $80,000.

I'll explain this with some examples:

Imagine you are only earning $8,000 a year. You will barely be able to afford food, let alone shelter, and you will likely be very stressed or living off other people by scavenging.

Now imagine you are earning $80,000 a year. You can afford a house, a car, to go out, have nice dinners, and gather some savings so you can afford medical bills or travel. You are able to freely donate to a charity of your choice. You can also court your next partner or enjoy a lil sexy time with your current one.

But now imagine you earn $800,000 a year. Your house might be bigger and you might fly first class instead of economy, but you are doing basically the same things as before but are working a lot harder and don't have as much time to spend with friends and family. Also, the sex isn't really going to get any better just because you have more money.

Now, earning $8 million a year, or $80 million a year, is pretty unlikely, and it's also an absurd amount of money usually acquired by making money with money, not from actually working harder or contributing more to society.

Bottom line, take care of your bills, necessities, stay out of the red and you will be feeling good in your life. If living a satisfactory life isn't good enough for you, good. Cue in the balancing act between your passion and your source of income.

I think the best piece of advice about following your passions and trying to make a living off of them came from Elizabeth Gilbert. In her book Big Magic, she speaks about letting your passions and what you love to do be just that. To not demand and apply stress to your passion by making financial demands.

I found the quickest way to lose your passion boner is by pressuring it to perform and produce money. Nothing kills a dream faster, nothing stops your creative juices faster than the impending doom of a financially stressful situation. Your passion or dream is not meant to sit there like a trained monkey and perform tricks for money. Not yet anyways.

Whenever people ask me if they should take a risk and quit their steady job to pursue their part time passion project, 99% of the time I say no. I have literally turned into Suze Orman.

Remember when people used to call in and she would weigh the pros and cons and the risk involved in peoples purchases and investments? I have turned into her. This is not because I don't believe in people and their dreams, its quite the opposite. I believe and care too much about people to encourage them to risk it and suffer.

Not everything you love needs to be making you money. Having expectations about anything, especially something you enjoy doing, is not productive. Like I said before life is too long. Quitting your job that is paying all your bills and then some to risk being without savings and stressed out about money is not worth it. What is worth it is a side hustle. Use your spare time, weekends, invest in a baby sitter or a nanny if you have kids to buy your time to work and perfect your passion project. This is productivity 2.0. If you can manage to buy yourself some time, freedom and resources, you have just got a gold star from me.

"Leverage what you have to get what you want."

Remember you are in it for the long game. The best way to be productive is to plan accordingly and responsibly. Nothing happens overnight. Your dreams don't deserve to be pressured because you need them to produce. There is no need to suffer when you are trying to pursue your passions.

This is a story as old as time and a limiting belief that plagues many. The artist has to be starving in order to create his best work. That is such bull shit. In order to create your best work your necessities must be met. In order to dream and be free, you must be free from worrying if you can pay your rent this month. It is very difficult to create abundance if you are surrounded by lack.

Did you know that Elizabeth Gilbert worked part time in a restaurant while she pursued her writing career? She still worked part time even after she wrote her now famous book, Eat, Pray, Love. She needed the stability of a steady paycheck in order to fully explore the freedom of her passions. Elizabeth didn't quit her part time job until the big check came in and Eat, Pray, Love got picked up and produced into a movie.

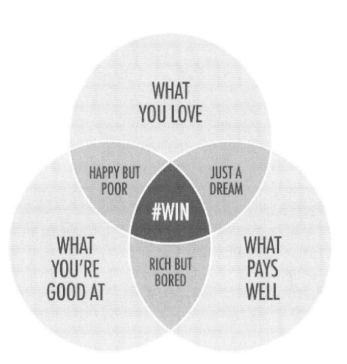

As you are sitting at a job you aren't in love with or hate passionately, ask yourself what are you learning. Part of being productive is taking a second to realize what you are learning from your current situation. In every job you have there is a skill you are honing to help you navigate your next venture. You are cultivating your personal tool box that you need in order to perform your dream and your passion to the best of your ability.

Each job I have had, has primed me for the career I have now. Even though I didn't necessarily like the jobs I was doing along the way, I was being productive and pulling out the pieces I needed in order to be successful for the full picture, the end game, the big show!

Think of your dream and passion as your masterpiece. Each masterpiece has many parts, many colors, shapes and they all take time.

My first career was working as a hairstylist and make up artist. I needed this job in my tool box to make sure my customer service skills were on point. There is nothing that tests your patience and self will more than applying ladies from Beverly Hills hair color. I learned how to listen and communicate with clients.

Working with this fickle genre of ladies was not easy by any means. I learned how to charm the most stuck up, snobby, entitled rich bitches and have them laughing and eating out of the palm of my hand by the end of their service. I learned how to be a people person even when all I wanted to do was drown them in the shampoo bowl or smother their baby blonde highlights with a fire engine red gloss.

From the Beverly Hills salon, I took my stellar customer service skills, love for music and reinvented myself as a Dj. Here I got a chance to learn a new skill, the art of performance. I learned how to entertain, find my personality and got over my fear of talking on a microphone. I also learned how to sell myself (services, not my body!) For the first few years I didn't have an agent and had to hit the pavement in search for gigs. This meant researching the right place, the right time and the right people to talk to.

I perfected my elevator pitch on who I was and what I was about. Being the shy little Canadian girl that I was, I had never learned how to talk about myself and certainly not in a positive, sell yourself type way. I always played small and never talked about myself or what I was capable of. Because I had no choice, I blossomed like a flower and enjoyed telling people what I was up to and what I could offer.

THE STRUGGLE YOU'RE FACING IS A TEST TO SEE IF YOU'RE TRULY COMMITTED TO THE LIFE YOU WANT.

Don't play small. Don't shrink yourself down because you are afraid others can't handle you, don't care what others have to say or who will judge you. Everyone has a story and journey that must be shared. Whether it's services you have to offer or an idea you have, spread the word.

Do This Now:

If you do not love what you do, create an exit strategy asap. This is your chance. This is your out. I know bills come and money is needed to survive. So this is the time to buckle down and figure out what you are passionate about and start creating opportunities to be productive. Get your priorities straight. Making money is not difficult, finding or creating a job is not difficult. Nothing will cause you more stress, anxiety and lead to depression faster than hating what you do and feeling like you must do it day in and day out for 8 plus hours a day. I know you have bills and responsibilities. So do I, so does everyone else in the world unless you're my dog.

Why are you doing something you don't want to do? Pretty simple. No one is forcing you to clock into your job every morning. No one is forcing you to be unhappy and miserable. You are choosing both. So if you do not like what you do, stop doing it. Start doing something you like and are passionate about.

Set a big picture goal. This can be anything you want, just make sure it is so big that it scares the living crap out of you. Above that big end game goal set some micro goals. Think lily pads to step on along the way.

Hire a coach

It doesn't matter what you do or what your job is hire a coach. If you are in a field you don't want to be in, hire a coach to help you figure out where you would like to be.

If you are happy in your job and want to further your business, hire a coach. Hiring a coach gets you the answers your looking for and beyond, faster! In most cases with a lot less stress and a lot less potential for losing time and money. Just like a trainer is for your health and body, a coach is for your business and other areas of expertise. They will motivate you, hold you accountable and demand action. That is the perfect recipe to be productive.

Join a mastermind or community group

Find a community of people within your industry or with the same passions as you who are actually out there doing what they are passionate about.

"Show me who your friends are and I'll tell you who you are." I love this quote and it is so true.

Your current friends are a reflection of you, and are 100% your choice. A friend is someone you chose to spend time and associate with. The people you choose to be around shape your personality, the way you think, the way you speak, and the way you perceive the world.

Whether we are aware of it or not, the people we choose to pay attention to and consider friends frame our reality. They are a barometer of what is normal and what is possible. It is difficult to learn to play basketball if you spend your days with a soccer team. The truth is, your choice of friends reflect the person you are today, and will in turn affect the person you will become tomorrow.

You should always be growing and the very best way to do that is by surrounding yourself with people who are doing the same.

FLAWSOME

NOUN

1. Flawed but awesome
2. A mark, fault, or other imperfection but extremely impressive.

Resources

5 Love Languages by Gary Chapman:

Dr. Gary Chapman identifies five basic languages of love and then guides couples towards a better understanding of their unique languages of love. Learn to speak and understand your mate's love language, and in no time you will be able to effectively love and truly feel loved in return. Skillful communication is within your grasp!

Big Magic by Elizabeth Gilbert:

With profound empathy and radiant generosity, Elizabeth Gilbert offers insight into the mysterious nature of inspiration. She asks us to embrace our curiosity and let go of needless suffering. She shows us how to tackle what we most love, and how to face down what we most fear. She discusses the attitudes, approaches, and habits we need in order to live our most creative lives. Balancing between soulful spirituality and cheerful pragmatism, Gilbert encourages us to uncover the "strange jewels" that are hidden within each of us. Whether we are looking to write a book, make art, find new ways to address challenges in our work, embark on a dream long deferred, or simply infuse our everyday lives with more mindfulness and passion, Big Magic cracks open a world of wonder and joy.

The Science of Getting Rich by Wallace D. Wattles:

The Science of Getting Rich is a classic and was published in 1910. Wattles passed away in 1911, shortly after publishing this book. It caused a sensation then, and continues to be popular today. In fact, Rhonda Byrne said that part of her inspiration for her best-selling book and film The Secret came from this book.

The timeless principles in this classic will transform your financial future.

You Are a Badass: How to Stop Doubting Your Greatness and Start Living an Awesome Life by Jen Sincero:

Sincero, a former skeptic herself, delivers the goods minus the New Age cheese, giving even the snarkiest of poo-pooers exactly what they need to get out of their ruts and start kicking some ass. By the end of You Are a Badass, you will understand why you are how you are, how to love what you can't change, how to change what you don't love, and how to start living the kind of life you used to be jealous of.

This isn't Good bye.
More of a, See you soon!

Let's stay connected:

Instagram @jessicajeboult & @asobergirlsguide

www.saveyourowndamnlife.com

www.asobergirlsguide.com

Printed in Great Britain
by Amazon

32741273R00084